What I Did for Money

Lucille Palis Finamore

What I Did *for* Money

Meetinghouse Books
PROVIDENCE PUBLISHING CORPORATION
Franklin, Tennessee

Copyright 2001 by Lulu Finamore

All rights reserved. Written permission must be secured from the publisher to use or reproduce any part of this book, except for brief quotations in critical reviews or articles.

Printed in the United States of America

05   04   03   02   01   1   2   3   4   5

Library of Congress Catalog Card Number: 2001096721

ISBN: 1-57736-249-7

Cover design by Gary Bozeman

Illustrations on pages 6, 17, 54, 74, 112, and 115 by Lynn Thompson

Illustration on page 99 by Virginia Queller

Author photo by Jeff Haynie

The stories in *What I Did for Money* are based on the author's experience, but names of businesses, locales, and persons have been changed to preserve confidentiality and protect identities.

Meetinghouse Books
PROVIDENCE PUBLISHING CORPORATION
238 Seaboard Lane • Franklin, Tennessee 37067
800-321-5692
www.providencepubcorp.com

Find Happiness in the Garden

Spend time in the garden,
Not to escape but to discover.
Discover science, chemistry, and botany.
Grow in peace and solitude in the garden.
Fragrance, color, and texture are there.
Enjoy the warmth of the summer sun.
Smell the pungent fragrance of the chrysanthemums
As autumn falls over the garden.
Feel the stillness and quiet as winter covers the plants
In a frosting of snow.
Share in the miracle of growth.
Working in the garden is best done on one's knees
In humble gratitude.
The life of man began in a garden;
The fruits of the garden have kept man alive.
The garden is where man and his creator become one.

Wayne Suite and LuLu Finamore

Contents

Preface and Acknowledgments	ix
Impossible Dream	1
Bidding War for Mother's Home	8
One Size Does Not Fit All	9
Trust Your Broker	12
Whatever It Takes	29
The Psychology of Selling Real Estate	30
The Cat and Mouse Game	42
It's All In the Family	68
A Gift of a Deal	70
The Three-year Contract	88
No Mortgage	101
Move Number Nine	102
About the Author	118

Preface and Acknowledgments

In the early 1970s the price of one of the first houses I sold was thirty-five thousand dollars. By selling two homes a month the commission was approximately twelve thousand dollars in my first year. Today selling *one*, one-million-dollar home will result in more commission than I made in my entire first year of selling real estate. If you sell your own listing that figure will almost double.

When I first became a realtor associate there was no designation such as a "million dollar salesperson." In Sunday's newspaper there was a full page, with colored photos, of realtor associates who sold properties totaling millions of dollars. Five associates sold ten million dollars or more of real estate, four sold eight million dollars or more, and sixteen sold six million dollars or more. In addition, there were 134 multimillion-dollar sales professionals from this one office! The realtor has four hundred independent contractors in fourteen offices.

Million-dollar homes are no longer unheard of or unusual. It may be a fifty-year-old home on Ridgewood Avenue in Glen Ridge, New Jersey, a new home at Mocking Bird Hill in Brentwood, Tennessee, or on Bitter Bush in Truckee, California.

What will homes cost in the future? If you buy right I don't believe you can go wrong by investing in real estate. Real estate has been very good to me. It's a wonderful career. It's what I did to make money.

Now there is the Internet. One can avoid contact with another human by going to the web site www.realtor.com. I was amazed to find the array of homes that are available at the click of a key. Zero in on the state, then the community, the price, number of bedrooms and baths and there you have a selection of homes.

But the internet will never take the place of another human being. The picture cannot tell you if the den or TV room has a wall large enough for your entertainment unit, if there is an area for your six-foot leather sofa, or if the children's bedrooms are separate from the master bedroom area. It probably will not list what the taxes are or the cost of the utilities.

My friends were very thoughtful, helpful, and gentle with their suggestions when they read my short stories.

Thank you Sharyn Pelych, Paula Harris, Debbie Finamore Laffey, Martha Reber, Gloria Oliver, Sandra Wills, and Victor Judge of Vanderbilt University.

Victor, your gentle suggestions, enthusiastic encouragement, and the delightful way you acknowledged the form of a special thought or phrase are what encouraged me to publish my short stories.

CHAPTER 1

Impossible Dream

I was sitting in my real estate office wondering where my next lead might come from when the phone rang. "Opportunity Realtors, how may I help you?"

A woman's shy, shaky voice said, "I would like to buy a house."

This sounded fine to me since I was in the business of selling houses. The woman on the other end of the line sounded weak and frail, or maybe insecure. I hesitated to ask the needed questions.

"I'll be happy to help you. I'll need to ask a few personal questions."

"Okay."

"How many are in your family?" I was trying to find out how many bedrooms she would need.

"Just my husband, my daughter, and myself. Oh, my brother also lives with me. He has multiple sclerosis. The therapist comes a few times a week to exercise him."

"Then there are four of you?"

"Yes ma'am."

I thought three bedrooms would be enough, so I continued with my questions.

"What does your husband do for a living? What is his income?" I was trying to make conversation and get more than one-word answers.

"He," there was a slight pause. "He is a disabled veteran. He has a 100 percent disability." I have sold homes to vets before but never to a disabled one.

"He does not work at all?" I wanted to make sure there was no income from a part-time or under-the-table job.

"No ma'am."

This sounds like a problem. The G.I. Bill allows a veteran to purchase property without a down payment but a non-working vet? I needed more information.

"Do you work?"

"Yes, I do."

Still the short answers, not much conversation. I felt as if I were invading her privacy.

"What do you do for a living?" In my job, as a professional real estate salesperson, I have to find out as much personal information as possible. Not just to be curious, but to be able to qualify the buyer. The amount of money coming in is very important. From this I can compute how much income can go for taxes, mortgage, insurance, heat, and repairs. So far, nothing was coming in. You can't go too far on that.

"What do you do for a living?" I asked again.

This shy, little voice said, "When I tell you, you probably will not want to sell me a house."

This was 1974 in what was referred to as a blue-collar working town. The majority of women were still at-home wives or mothers. They washed on Monday, ironed on Tuesday, and on Thursday and Friday cleaned the house for the weekend. They shopped on Saturday for food so they could prepare a *big* Sunday dinner. Family always came to visit on Sunday. Then the week started all over again.

Obviously, this could not be the case here. This woman had to make money somehow. Remembering what she said when I asked her what work she did, I wondered what it was. Like a flash it came to me. She must be a prostitute! What else could she do that she would be ashamed of? I felt embarrassed to go on asking questions, and yet I had to have more information. How would I know if she could afford a house if

I did not know how much money she earned? I really had to know where the money came from and if it was a steady income. I was getting very embarrassed, and I didn't know how to get the needed information. Oh well, plunge forward!

Very hesitantly I asked again, "What *do* you do for a living?" I almost did not want to hear what she would say.

This very quiet voice said in a whisper, "I'm a meter maid."

There was a short pause for a deep breath. "You're a meter maid? I don't understand. What is it that you do?"

"I check the parking meters and give out tickets."

I felt so guilty. I thought this person was some vulgar, in my mind, immoral creature. She turned out to be someone who was trying, in her small way, to uphold the local parking regulations for the police department and support a family.

"What is so bad about that?" I asked.

"People are so nasty to me. When they find me writing up a ticket, some people swear at me. I had a man spit at me."

This woman's voice was so humble and meek I was embarrassed that the thought of "prostitute" had even slithered into my judgmental mind. When she assured me that she had a steady job with the police department, and had in fact been on the force for six years, I arranged for an appointment.

Her price range was very limited—thirty-five to forty thousand dollars. The down payment was one thousand dollars. I told her I could arrange for a no-down-payment loan. She could have the one thousand dollars for the attorney's fee. There really was very little to select from. Our appointment was for Friday, but on Thursday I had not found any property that fit the bill for them. In the afternoon I called her. "Mary, I have to cancel our appointment for tomorrow. I haven't found anything in your price range."

"Oh, I hope you aren't going to be like the other realtors."
"What do you mean?"
"I've called quite a few offices, but when I give them the information they want, I never get a call back."

Now I understood why she was so slow in giving me the information. Her voice sounded so sad. I felt sorry for her. Her husband, Ralph, was a man who went into the service for his country and came out a broken person. Now, no one could find a house for his family and him.

"Mary, I promise I will find something for you. It will probably take a little time. There has to be something out there for you."

She sounded a little choked up, as if she was going to cry. "Give me the weekend to look at what is available and I'll call you Monday. Okay?"

In that very soft, pitiful voice she said, "I'll wait for your call. Ralph will be here to take the message."

Now that I've made a commitment, how am I going to keep it? There has to be some houses in the less desirable areas that are well kept. I had two appointments that kept me busy on Saturday. Sunday I spent time in the office looking through the multiple listing book trying to find something I could show to them on Monday. I found two properties that she might be able to afford. Both were in what would be called a rather depressed area. Our little town, population of fifty-two thousand, had the park section, which was the newer section and was the most expensive area. There was also the Polish Church area, where the Polish immigrants had settled; the Ampere area where the Italian and Jewish families lived; and the south end area where the factories were located. I guess most towns are divided more or less in this way. The greater distance between the industries and the residential properties the more expensive they become.

Impossible Dream

Monday I called and Ralph took the message. They would meet me at the address I gave him at four o'clock. I had the house open, the lights on, and was waiting at the door for them. Mary was very thin with dark circles under her eyes. The teenage daughter was quiet. I could tell immediately that Mary was not happy with what I had selected for her. But then, it was what they could afford. She told me there was not enough room and asked, "Where will I put my brother, who is in a wheelchair?" She hadn't shared this information with me before. Her husband was very thin and looked helpless. There was no way he would be able to do any work on a house. His skin had a yellow tint. He looked very unhealthy. I could tell he was on medication that slowed him down. Even his speech was a little slurred.

I was later to find out that he was an alcoholic. The daughter was in high school. Mary wanted something better for her family. What a sad situation. I promised to get back to her. But my dilemma was, what they could afford they did not like!

I did a little research and found out that a vet, with 100 percent disability, does not have to pay real estate taxes. This made all the difference. Now they would be able to afford a little more expensive home. I knew of one in the Ampere section that an elderly lady had owned. It was in fairly good condition. She had died, and it was part of her estate. The heirs wanted to sell and divide the spoils. Usually in situations like this, the heirs will place an unrealistic price on the property. The house will sit on the market for months while the estate pays the taxes, electric, heat, and insurance bills. We were lucky! In this case the heirs were very cooperative and accepted a realistic price.

At the closing, Mary had the biggest smile on her face. The circles under her eyes had almost disappeared. She thanked me for working with her and not brushing her aside

as had happened to her so often. Mary and her family moved in. Her brother enjoyed sitting in his wheelchair on the front porch. The therapist came to exercise him a few times a week. The daughter went to a new high school. The father was home with his emotional problems and pain. Every day Mary went to work.

In snow, rain, and cold she did her job. I don't know if anyone else cursed at her or spit on her. Every so often, on my way to show a house, I saw Mary. Each time I saw her at her job as meter maid, she looked more emaciated. I would wave and she would slowly wave back. One time we spoke and she told me the kitchen was being painted. She seemed to be content.

A few years went by and one day her daughter called to tell me that her mother had died. I went to the wake. I cried a little. The disabled neurotic husband, the daughter, and Mary's sister were there. Her brother had died the year before. They each told me how happy Mary had been because I was able to find her a home. Her sister told me it had been Mary's "impossible dream." How could she ever own a house without money for a down payment and a husband who was 100 percent disabled?

CHAPTER 2

Bidding War for Mother's Home

And then there was the sale of our mother's home in 1975, after she moved into a nursing home. It was a six-room colonial with one-and-a-half bathrooms. We were asking eighteen thousand dollars for the property.

My brother Joe and I held an open house on a Saturday afternoon. A few people walked through the house, but two of her neighbors seemed interested. While the five of us stood in the dining room we learned that one neighbor was a real estate agent and the other neighbors were a husband and wife who wanted their son to live nearby. Suddenly they started to make verbal offers. They were trying to outbid one another by one-hundred-dollar increments.

Can you imagine a bid of $18,100 by the real estate agent?

The other neighbors then offered $18,200 with an emphasis on the two hundred dollars.

The real estate agent jumped his offer up to $18,400. I guess he thought a jump of two hundred dollars would sound impressive.

The husband and wife looked at each other, hesitated for a moment, and then he stepped forward and very slowly but strongly bid $18,500. The real estate agent declined to go any higher.

The house was sold for $18,500, and all the money was spent to keep Mother comfortable at a nursing home.

CHAPTER 3

One Size Does Not Fit All

Patty called my office looking to buy a house in the price range of $120,000. She sounded knowledgeable and was anxious to move from her parents' home. I made an appointment to show Patty, Mark, and their daughter, Melissa, a small two-bedroom house. We were meeting at the property. When I saw them struggling to get out of their compact car, I realized this house was not for them. He was six-foot-three and weighed about 250 pounds. She was five-foot-ten and weighed about 160 pounds. Once in the house, they indicated that the living room, dining room, and kitchen were adequate. But when we went to the master bedroom I knew we had a problem. The four of us could not fit in the bedroom all at the same time. I stayed in the hall and apologized. It's hard to tell a person's size over the phone.

We met several more times and I showed them other one-family houses, but there was always a problem with the location, condition, or size. At a later time I did sell them a two-family house with large rooms. They were able to afford it because the house needed some tender loving care and would not sell for top dollar. The rent would help them with the mortgage payments.

While their mortgage application was being processed, Mark unexpectedly stopped by my office. I observed this six-foot-three man walking in, with shoulders bent and a questioning look on his face. "What's wrong, Mark?"

In a soft voice he asked, "Will it make a difference with the bank, for our mortgage, if I lost my job?"

What a question! How can you make mortgage payments without a job? I kept my thoughts to myself.

"Let's go into the conference room." This man who had been loud and sure of himself a week ago was a pussycat today. "Tell me what happened."

"Ya know we're building the stadium, and the concrete work is done. So I got laid off."

I took a deep breath, wondering if this difficult sale was going to fall apart. "Will more concrete work have to be done next week or the week after?"

"Sure, but now I don't have a job." He hesitated for a moment, "And there is something else I didn't put on the mortgage application. I pay alimony to my ex-wife."

"You will probably have to show that on the application." He still had an odd look on his face. I was almost afraid to ask, "Is there anything else?"

"Yes."

I guess he wasn't happy to tell me because I had to say, "What is it?"

"I served time."

"Oh, God!" I couldn't help myself; it just burst out of me. "Is there anything else?"

He was very embarrassed and answered, "No."

I really did not want to ask, but I had to know. "What were you in for?"

"Numbers. I had to take the rap for someone higher up."

"I will look at the mortgage application to see if you must reveal the information about your arrest." I wondered for a moment if this was an excuse to get out of the contract. "Do you still want the house?"

"You bet! I've got to get away from my in-laws."

He spoke with such feeling, I knew he was desperate to leave. The father-in-law was a fantastic handyman. Whatever his wife asked for, he was able to provide, and she was a wonderful housekeeper. Their home was meticulous, with a new bathroom and a new kitchen.

"All right, let's hold off for awhile before we panic. If they call you back next week, get in touch with me." I knew the stadium was far from finished, and I was sure he would have a job, through the union, very soon.

He did get called back to work. They were approved for the mortgage and we had a closing on the two-family house. His wife went back to work at the telephone company so they would have a steady income and benefits.

Two years later they called me to list their house for sale. When I arrived at the property I saw that all the little neglected things were still neglected. Tender loving care was still necessary, but the new owners would be the ones to provide it. Mark and Patty were fortunate that real estate values had increased, and therefore they were able to gain a small profit.

Now I understood why the association with his fastidious, hardworking in-laws was not a happy one.

CHAPTER 4

Trust Your Broker

It was my "opportunity time," as they say in real estate, when it is your time to answer incoming calls. I find it very interesting. You never know who is on the other end of the line. I've had mothers call for their busy adult children, neighbors call to find out the price of the house next door, and some people call knowing full well they can not afford the house.

"Good morning Opportunity Realtors, how may I help you?"

I heard a young man say, "Ya know that house on Main Street?" His voice was a little gruff, but he sounded young.

I had a house listed for sale on that street so I said, "Do you mean the one with our sign in the front yard?" Main Street runs for almost the full length of the Brook section and there are about ten "For Sale" signs posted there.

"Yea, that's where I got this number. I heard from a friend that it could be bought for fifty-nine thousand dollars." This particular spring market was a buyer's market, but fifty-nine thousand dollars for a house in that area hasn't been heard of in eighteen or twenty years!

"I think your friend is wrong. By the way, what is your name?"

"I'm Tony."

"Hi Tony, my name is LuLu. I think you mean $159,000."

"No, my friend said they had an offer for fifty-nine thousand dollars and they took it. Only the deal fell apart."

In my twenty years of experience, I have found that neighborhood talk is usually incorrect when it comes to prices. Tony went on to explain that his friend had just bought a house two doors away.

"I don't know where this fifty-nine-thousand-dollar price came from, but believe me, it is not correct. As a matter of fact, I just listed this house. Prior to now it had been listed with another office for $179,000. You can't even buy a lot in this area for fifty-nine thousand dollars."

"Hey come off it, that house needs a lot of work."

"You are right, it needs some work, but it has a wonderful piece of property. It's over four hundred feet deep."

"Yea, that's what I need."

I was happy to hear that. "Would you like to take a look at it now?"

"Can you meet me *now*?" He seemed surprised that I was available.

"I'll meet you in fifteen minutes, at eleven o'clock." He agreed to be there. I made arrangements for someone else to answer the phone. I was working for a large corporation. The phones were covered from nine in the morning until eight in the evening. While I drove the short distance, I wondered why he needed a large piece of property. I knew the house needed work and wondered if he was handy.

When I drove up to the property, Tony was waiting for me in his clean black Corvette. He was a strikingly handsome, slim Neapolitan type, with a ruddy tan complexion, short well-groomed black hair, and a beautiful smile. Hand extended, he greeted me as he said, "I'm Tony."

As we shook hands I thought, "He must have no trouble dating." Before our interview was over, I learned he had just broken off his engagement, was a landscaping architect, had a car phone and a beeper, and he and the bank owned the landscaping equipment he used in his business.

I walked him through the vacant house that still contained a few odds and ends of old furniture. After he finished making comments about the dirty carpeting, the cracks in the ceiling, and the watermarks on the TV room ceiling, I said, "Well, what do you think?"

"The property is perfect. I need it for my equipment, but the house needs a lot of work."

"Not really. The kitchen and the bathroom are very good, but the old soiled carpeting has to come up and all the rooms need painting."

Then he started again with the story about fifty-nine thousand dollars. I told him to forget about that. Someone did not have the correct information. Tony was about twenty-five years old and had never owned a house. I realized it was necessary for me to educate him, as we say in the business.

"Tony, this house was put on the market over two years ago for $210,000." I emphasized the price.

"Forget it, that's ridiculous!"

"No, Tony, two-and-a-half years ago the market had hit its highest peek. That's when the owner died and his two sons put it up for sale. If it had been in tip-top condition they would have gotten close to that price." I went on to explain that for the last few years the market had gone in only one direction, and that was down. We, in the business, estimate prices have decreased at a rate of 1 to 1½ percent a month, that is 12 to 18 percent a year. At a minimum of 12 percent a year for two years, that is 24 percent. "This property," I said, "has depreciated over forty-five thousand dollars. That brings the price to about $165,000."

I thought he was either deaf or stubborn because he said, "Offer him sixty-nine thousand dollars."

"Tony, they are not going to take it! But I will talk to them. Are you ready to give me a deposit?" It was ridiculous, but I had to whet his appetite. He had a very appealing way about him. I couldn't just drop him. I knew he needed a place to store his valuable equipment so he would be able to make his monthly payments to the bank.

"Sure, how much do you want?"

"How about a thousand dollars?" That's how it all began.

The owners were two brothers. They both lived out of town and had their own businesses and family obligations. Bob lived three quarters of an hour to the west and Bill a half hour south of their late father's property. The two of them could never find time to clean out and freshen up the property. It was very difficult to reach them by phone. The weekend came and went. I kept trying to reach either one of them without luck. Tony called me twice a day to find out if I had contacted them. Monday morning at seven, before I showered, I tried once more. I really don't like to call before eight in the morning or after ten in the evening. But I had no choice.

"Hello," I heard an obviously sleepy male say.

"Hi, this is your realtor. I'm sorry to wake you, but I've been trying to reach you since Friday."

"We go to Pennsylvania for the weekends. I hope you're calling about an offer."

"I am."

But before I could say anything else he said, "It better be a good one."

That took the joy out of my day. I had a visual picture of him swinging his legs over the side of the bed, ready for a really good offer. "It's a low-ball offer."

"If it's less than $159,000 I don't even want to hear it."

That really shook me up because, when the brothers listed the property they had not asked for my professional opinion as to the price. When they called to list the house, I informed them I had shown it a few times to an attorney. They told me at what price they wanted to list the property. They did not want a comparable analysis done to show the price trend. Sellers do not list their property at the exact price they will accept from a buyer. So I was a little taken back.

"You mean you expect to get the listed price?" Almost all buyers expect a little play in the price.

"We have already reduced it from $210,000. The price is $159,000. See what you can do."

He sounded gruff and unyielding. I felt intimidated. I thought this was not the time to pursue the price issue. I really had nothing to offer, but I had to make an attempt at it. He added that if they didn't get their price then they would rent it. That was the end of the conversation.

It was news to me that they would consider renting. The house needed to be decorated inside and out. They would have to empty the entire house. The grounds were unkempt and the aluminum siding needed attention. The interior had no appeal. By talking to the brothers and the neighbors I learned that the mother had died first and the father two years later. The brothers did not have the time or the interest to do what was needed to make it saleable.

With a little imagination it was easy to see that tender loving care, plus some money and hard work, would turn it into a lovely three-bedroom home. The kitchen and bath were modern and there was a TV room. Local and New York City buses were at the front door, a plus, if you needed them and a minus if you didn't, because the street was busy. It did have a wonderful rear property. I could think of all the pluses and minuses and I knew someone could do magic with this property. I wanted it to be Tony. But his knowledge of real estate was zero.

At half past seven Tony was on the phone. "Well, did you get the guy?"

"Tony, they know only one number and that is $159,000."

"Forget it, what else do you have?"

"Tell me exactly what you need and what you can spend."

Then the story started to unravel. When he was in his teens he worked for a gardener who lived a few doors away from this property. I interrupted and said, "I sold the house to him."

"He kept his gardening equipment on the property and worked out of his house. The neighbors didn't mind his equipment coming and going. That's why I like that area."

Tony realized because of the depth of the property a two-car garage could easily be built there. This would work fine for him. It was perfect except for the price.

"What I really need is a two- or three-bedroom house with a two- or three-car garage for about $130,000. I want to stay in this general area."

"Do you have time to look at some property this afternoon?" We decided to meet at my office at half past eleven. I sat down at my home computer and started to pull up the properties with his land requirements. They were not in the area he wanted. Then I pulled up houses in the $130,000 to $140,000 price ranges. It was eight o'clock and I had most of my day in motion. I showered and had breakfast, all the while thinking, "I know the Main Street property is good for him. If only I can convince him he will not find what he is looking for at the price he wants to spend."

Tony was right on time for his appointment. He looked great. As he walked down the hall to the conference room, the beautiful black shiny hair and a happy smile made a few heads turn to take a second look. I had photo copies ready of all the houses I had pulled up on the computer. I arranged them first by lot size, then by price from $130,000 to $140,000. As he looked at the pictures and saw the addresses, he rejected each one.

"I told you I didn't want to be down in that area." He was very emphatic when he said this.

"Tony, there are only two areas in town where you will get large lots so you can park your vehicles. One is where the house for $159,000 is and the other is where you don't want to be."

"Okay, then I'll rent where my trucks are for now. But I still want a house. My accountant said I need a write off."

Now I knew the real reason for the necessity of a house! He has been so successful that he needs a write off. I have heard this quite a few times from buyers to whom I have sold homes. I was happy he was doing so well. "This will be his driving force, if only he can get realistic about the price of property," I thought.

"Great! Now that we have eliminated the large lots, here are the houses in the price range you indicated." I handed him a set of photos and information on each house.

The reaction was evident on his face. He looked me right in the eyes and very emphatically said, "I do not want a Cape Cod!"

At this point I decided I had to zero in on the house he made the ridiculous offer on. But I knew I could not push him. His masculine ego would not allow that. I would have to try my "real estate psychology."

We went over the pictures again. "Tony, this is the picture you said looked like a nice house. Let's go see it. This next one is a little more expensive than you indicated you would pay, but let's take a look at it any way." He agreed to look and I made three appointments.

In the first house, the dining room was too small. The second one was in a crowded location. The last house, priced at $169,000 really made him flip!

"The yard is small, the house is small, and the condition ain't that much better than the one your guy wants $159,000 for."

I made my point! My psychology was working. "So, I guess the one on Main Street is worth $159,000."

Very vehemently he said, "No, I'll offer $139,000 and that's it!" I suggested we go to the office to draw up a contract for that price.

Tony said, "I have to go to one of my jobs to see how the guys are doing. I'll be at your office at half past three." He was smiling that broad clean smile. Extending his hand he said, "Do ya think we have a chance at $139,000?"

I smiled back and assured him I would do the best I could. "I'll tell the owners you are sincere in your offer. Since the house is empty you will take title as quickly as possible. Another plus on your side, Tony, is that you do not have any property to sell." I went on to explain what else would be required. "The only contingencies in the contract will be the usual engineering, termite, and mortgage inspections."

The last time I spoke to Bob, I told him how difficult it was to reach him and he gave me his beeper number. In anticipation of Tony signing the contract, I decided to call Bob to see if he and his brother would be able to meet me at my office that evening. It happened to be my night to play bridge. I had an obligation to present the offer as expeditiously as possible. In a brisk market, which we were not in, if I were to delay presenting the offer someone else might come in before me and the property could be gone. I would be in deep trouble if that ever happened. This I did not need. I dialed the beeper number, left my number, and started to put the offer together while I waited for Bob to call. Through previous conversations I learned that they would hold a small mortgage. Tony would be putting down $13,900, which is 10 percent. The brothers would hold 10 percent and the bank would grant an 80 percent mortgage. I put a quick occupancy in the contract, since there was nothing for Tony to sell. I knew this would appeal to the sellers. I heard my name over the office intercom. I was sure it was Bob returning my call. "This is LuLu how may I help you?"

It was Tony. "Hi LuLu, today is Friday, and I had to pay my men off. Have you got the contract ready?"

"By the time you get here it will be. When you're here, do you want to talk to our financial service representative?"

"Good idea, see ya."

I finished typing the contract and went to find out if the representative had time to see Tony. As it turned out she did. When I got back to my desk there was another call for me. This time it was Bob. I told him that a buyer was coming in shortly to make an offer. "I would like to meet with you and your brother this evening."

He said that this evening was out of the question. He and his brother planned to be at the property on Saturday to clean out some of the leftover items. "We'll meet you at the office at ten o'clock." That saved my bridge game.

Tony arrived at my office at about half past three and I went over all the details of the contract with him. When he had no more questions, I asked him if he was ready to sign. "Sure, when do I get my answer?" I explained that the owners would be in town the next day. With a very serious note of authority in his voice he said, "Now, no one else can look at this house and make an offer, right?"

"Wrong, Tony. Until all parties have signed and both attorneys have approved the contracts, anyone can make an offer."

"Oh s____. Excuse me. You better hurry up and talk to those guys."

"As soon as they get to the office I'll let you know what they say." I did not want to burst his bubble and go into all the other pitfalls that can happen before one goes to a closing.

The representative and Tony went into her private office to go over the mortgage details and to prequalify him for the loan. This is one of the advantages a buyer or a seller has in working with a large office. The buyer knows what price range he can afford and the seller knows the buyer will qualify for the mortgage. At five o'clock I left the office.

The evening of bridge and dessert was great. By one o'clock I was in bed with happy thoughts of a sale and a commission, but I quickly wiped that out of my mind. A sale is not a sale until it is closed. That's why in this business, you can't spend the money until it's in your hot little hands.

The next day, at ten o'clock, the brothers were in my office. We sat down to talk and they confirmed that they had one offer but it fell apart. As we talked, they didn't seem anxious to get rid of the property. They both agreed to rent if necessary. I couldn't tell if they were trying to intimidate me or if they were unaware that we were in a buyer's market. When I told them the price being offered was $139,000 they both shook their heads, looked at each other, and Bob said, "It's not acceptable."

"He's a ready buyer. There's nothing to hold up a fast sale, no property to be sold." They were still shaking their heads. "If I were able to get $145,000 would you take it?"

This time Bill spoke. "No, $159,000 is the price."

I assured them that I would continue to try to get the best price possible. I also reiterated that we were in a very slow market. I felt that it was my obligation to tell them that there were not a lot of buyers out there. Their continued response was, "Then we will rent." I again pointed out the problems with tenants and that they would have to spend a considerable amount of money to decorate the whole house and have the gardener do the four hundred feet of gardening. I explained that property values were dropping, even giving examples of nearby house values that had depreciated in the last year. But all they said was, "Then we'll rent." They either were oblivious of the economy or very stubborn. They didn't know how lucky they were that someone was interested in their property. The house was neglected, it needed work, and the yard work was overpowering. I decided I had done the very best I could; now it was up to the buyer. Does he want this property or not? I called Tony on his beeper. He got back to me in five minutes.

I could hear the excitement in his voice. "Well did they take it?" Now comes the hard part, to tell someone his or her offer has been turned down after what they thought was a good price. Part of my real estate psychology is to have the buyer feel there is a light at the end of the tunnel.

"No, Tony, they didn't."

"What's wrong with them?" I could hear the anger in his voice. "That house needs so much work. I'm going to take another look at it with a builder friend of mine. I think maybe I'm overpaying."

"Come on Tony, you know the house has a good kitchen and bathroom. The land is perfect for you. There is nothing in this area, even in the $180,000 price range with property of this size." I paused to let it sink in. "The brothers said they want $159,000. I guess you're going to have to give it to them if you want this property."

"Well I think it's too much money." I could hear the indignation in his voice. "I'm going away this weekend. I'll call you Monday. Maybe I'll take a second look. Okay?"

I knew he was very frustrated. "That's fine with me. Maybe the brothers will talk about it over the weekend." I had to give him a little hope.

Monday morning at eight o'clock my home phone rang. "Am I calling too early?"

"Oh no, Tony, I work from eight to eight or even to nine or ten. What's up?" Whoever said real estate is an easy business has never lived it. It is seven days a week, some days twelve hours. When it's slow you work more hours, not to miss anything. When you're busy, the follow-up and keeping the buyer and seller happy takes over your life. It never fails that the day I decide to take a few hours off or plan a vacation all hell breaks loose.

"Did anything come on the market that I might be interested in?"

"I haven't turned my computer on yet, Tony."

"Well see if there is. My friend and I would like to take another look, around eleven o'clock. Okay?"

You have to be ready day or night when the mood hits. "Sure Tony, I'll call you on your beeper and let you know what I have for you."

"Good."

"I'll run out to see the new listings. I'll find out if there is something for you."

At the computer, I pulled up the new listings and looked for anything that might fit the bill for Tony. He was a ready buyer who made himself available to look at properties. It was my job to keep him interested in looking. Since I felt that Main Street was the best property available at this time for his requirements, I had to keep him looking and comparing until he convinced himself that Main Street was the right property. This is what I call the psychology of selling real estate.

Nothing came on the market that met his requirements at the price he was ready to pay. As a matter of fact, even more expensive homes did not have all his requirements. In any event, I put together a few houses. I ran out to see if there were any surprises. As the saying goes, "You can't tell a book by its cover." This is really true about houses. There were no surprises. Properties were all too small, too close together, or had small kitchens. He would give me all the same rejections as before. It was almost half past eleven, so I went to the office and called him on his beeper. I left my number and waited. As always, he called right back.

"Hi, LuLu, you got something good for me?" He was always so up and happy. How can I burst his bubble?

"Do you still want your friend to see the house on Main Street?"

"Why?" His voice got lower and the words were slower. "There's nothing else?"

"Oh, I could show you a few things. Let's meet at Main Street."

"Okay, fifteen minutes."

I arrived at the house five minutes before they did. As I looked around, I noted the cracks in the living room ceiling. The old wall-to-wall carpet had been taken out but the floors were dull. The water stains on the ceiling in the TV room were still there, as were odd pieces of old furniture. It really did look like a mess. But, nothing is perfect. The room size was good, the kitchen had nice cabinets, the bathroom was modern, the TV room, or office, was a plus. The property, the four-hundred-foot lot, was really what he was buying.

When Tony pulled up in his Corvette, his friend had a little trouble getting out of the car. I thought, "Oh no, his friend is someone I have known for a long time. We don't mesh. He's a smart aleck type who thinks the world is at his command." We kept the conversation to a minimum. This so-called builder started through the house pointing out all of the obvious problems, the cracks, the water stains, the dirty floors, and the busy street. I held back, not defending each fault. When he finished looking at the entire house, I agreed to the obvious problems. Then I asked him, "Where can you find Tony a house in this neighborhood, with the property he needs, at a price he can afford?" I paused. He had no answer. "There is nothing." I let this sink in and then said, "Tony, why don't you talk everything over. Give it real serious consideration, because I have nothing else to show you. While you wait, someone else may come along with an offer and knock you out of the box. Don't take too long."

Tony and his friend went outside. Needless to say his friend found more faults. I locked up the house and met them at the rear of the property. We talked about putting in a pool and a garage for his trucks. I knew this property was for him. Now he had to make up his mind. The friend was still finding fault.

"The aluminum siding at the peak is loose," he commented.

"I'll see you Tony." I decided the best thing I could do was to leave. "Give me a call when you decide what you want to do." I had reached the end of trying to persuade him that this was the best he could do.

The next day I had a call. "Okay lets go! Make the contract for $155,000. I'll put 10 percent down. Ask them to hold 10 percent. They better be happy with this price because I ain't goin' no higher!" Now he was a driven buyer! He finally decided he wanted this property.

"Very good! I'll get the owners together and present the contract. When can you come in to initial the changes?"

"Just call them and tell them that I raised the price."

There was no way I would make a verbal offer to the seller. I had done this once when I was new in the business. The seller had accepted the increase in the price. The next morning when the buyer came in to sign the new price he had decided, overnight, that he had gone up too high. I had to go back to the seller with a lower price. He was very angry with me and sold it to someone else.

"No, Tony, that is not the way it's done. You come in and initial the changes. Then, I will present the contract."

"Has anyone been looking at this property?"

When buyers are interested in a property, there comes a time when the thought of someone else also having the same interest spurs them into taking that final step.

"Tony, there are over one hundred offices in this board of realtors and more than a thousand sales people. It gets shown periodically."

"Okay, okay, I'll meet you at the office in a half hour."

As soon as I reached my office I called the brothers and asked them to be at my office in two hours.

"Don't forget, we're not budging on the price," was the response.

"Why did he have to say that?" I thought. I was feeling so confident now that Tony had finally made a good offer. One never knows what is in the seller's mind. I went in to see the financial service representative to find out what type of mortgage was available for a young self-employed buyer. There was a no-income-verification loan available that the representative could put him into. Mortgages are a whole other story and I did not want to get involved. All I wanted to know was if there was any money available.

Tony came in on time and, as usual, a few heads turned to follow him to my office. I had the contracts ready and he initialed the changes I was required to make.

"Now don't forget to tell them that I'm only putting down 10 percent because the house needs a lot of work. Don't let them tell you it's worth more money. I'm overpaying as it is. It's because of the land that I'm going this high."

"Okay Tony, don't worry. I'll tell them all of the faults you have complained to me about. Then I will tell them that you are a young man trying to be a success in your business." I wanted to tell him that they would be crazy if they didn't take his offer, but I had no right to second-guess the sellers.

"You'll call me as soon as you have an answer? Call on the car phone." He left with that wonderful smile and a cocky stride as he said, "Wait until you see what I'm gonna do to that place!"

I wanted to say how I hoped he would get the house, but I was afraid that I would hear the owner tell me, "Well then, we'll rent it." In no time at all the brothers were at the office. They had never been too friendly. I couldn't tell if the two of them were not good friends or if they didn't like me. So I put on a friendly smile and greeted them. We went to the conference room and before I gave them the contract I said, "How long ago did your father die?" They looked at each other and agreed it was two and a half years ago. "It's been vacant all that time?"

"Yes, we had to get it emptied out and that's not easy. We both have families and our businesses to take care of." He hesitated, "Then for a while, one of the neighbors thought they would buy it. But yes, it's been empty for two years."

They were helping me with the groundwork but didn't even know it. As I started to take the contracts out of the folder I said, "This young man has no property to sell. The contract has no contingency for the sale of any property. You could have the house off your hands fairly quickly. No more heating, tax, and insurance bills as you have had for the last two and a half years."

I handed a contract to each of them. They looked at the price and then at one another. I held my breath as I waited. The older brother said, "We should have listed with you a long time ago."

"You mean you'll take it?" I tried not to act too surprised but I expected all kinds of resistance. I was very stunned.

"Yes, the closing date looks fine and the 10 percent on the loan is good. I'll take this over to my attorney." Bob was the older brother and he was the one I had always spoken to. Now he seemed to take control. As he signed, he said, "My lawyer doesn't live too far from me so I'll drop this off." I asked for the attorney's name and phone number. They stood up to go. They thanked me again and we shook hands.

Wonders never cease! Each transaction is different. I had anticipated trouble and was ready to remind them that this was the only written offer they had received in two and a half years and that the house and land were unkempt. I wanted to tell them they better take this offer. I didn't have to go through the litany of negatives. All my anxiety was for nothing. I dialed Tony's beeper as fast as I could. In ten minutes he was back to me.

"What happened, did they like my offer?" The excitement in his voice was wonderful to hear. His first house, the perfect property, and the challenge to fix it to his liking!

"Yes, Tony, they did!" I told him I was a little surprised. "I think they liked the interest rate you offered on the note they will be holding."

"Oh that's great! Wait 'til you see what I am going to do to that place!"

He was so excited. I could picture him walking around with his cell phone and that wonderful smile on his face. It made me feel great to know how happy he was!

Time went by and changes occurred. True to his word, he did wonders to "his" place.

CHAPTER 5

Whatever It Takes

And then there was the young wife who came alone to look at a few houses. I found the perfect house for her! It was clean, well maintained, had large rooms, and was built in the 1920s. The New York City bus was at the door. This was perfect for them since they worked in the city. Her husband came to see the house that evening and was also pleased with the property his wife was excited about. We went to look at the two-car garage at the rear of the lot. While standing in the center of the garage he questioned its depth. He thought it was too short for their 1972 car. This was not an unusual situation. When the older houses were built the cars were much smaller.

They both loved the house. He drove his car down the driveway and as he approached the garage he attempted to park the car, caddy-corner, in the garage! Some buyers will do anything to overcome an obstacle. They did buy the house and had the situation corrected, as many other owners had done.

When buyers find a house they want, they will do whatever it takes to make it work.

CHAPTER 6

The Psychology of Selling Real Estate

An acquaintance of many years called to tell me his mother had died and that her property in Nutley would have to be sold. "It is a little cluttered. But maybe you should take a look at the house and see what it might sell for." The caretaker would be moving out in a day or so. There was no rush to do anything.

"I'll go to my files and see the comparable properties that have sold recently. How does your time look for tomorrow afternoon about a quarter past three?"

"That sounds good LuLu. I have an appointment at half past four at my office. You know her house; see you there."

The exterior was cute. It was a miniature English Tudor. This was a house that needed tender love and care. The property was large. The house was on a busy street. I had sold several homes in the area and knew it was convenient to everything. The New York bus was at the door.

Paul was on time. He called my attention to the rear of the property, which was large and in need of a gardener. We walked up the driveway to the front of the house. I noticed that the drive was in need of repair. The house was typical for the area. It was built in the 1950s with nice oak wood trim, good hardwood floors, and an attractive brick fireplace. There were cracks in the ceilings and the floor did sag a little in one area. The size of the rooms was adequate and the style was cute. But the furniture was too big for the dining room. It made the room look cramped. The one bedroom had a huge, king-sized bed with a large high headboard. The house would show better if it was empty.

I suggested a price of $165,000, adding, "It would probably sell for $160,000."

He immediately brought up the fact that a house two doors away had sold for $189,000, and that it was the same house.

Fortunately, I had previewed that property when it was for sale. Of course it was not the same house. "Paul, that property was converted to a two-family house. It had two modern kitchens, two modern bathrooms, and a deck off the rear of the house. It also had a finished recreation room." Before he could say anything I added, "Your house has the potential of being a mother-daughter style, after all the work is done."

I knew he was not happy with the information I had just given to him. "I'll have to talk to my brother and I'll get back to you."

A week later he called. The family decided to add ten thousand dollars to the sales price I had suggested. At that particular time we were in a slow market, a buyer's market, as it was called. The multiple listing service my office belonged to had a membership of more than one hundred offices. Twelve hundred salespeople were all working to sell the overpriced properties that were for sale.

Depending on what is in an unoccupied house, sometimes it is better to remove everything. But how do you tell a lifelong friend his mother's furniture isn't right for the size of the rooms? I couldn't. I hoped as I made a few suggestions he would understand. Maybe in time he will remove some furniture or have a "house sale."

A young man had rented the furnished rooms on the second floor. It really was a mess! The family had gone through the storage areas to see if the deceased had saved or hidden anything of value. Everything was thrown around.

The basement was not finished. There were old filing cabinets, a broken down washing machine, old clothes, and the bathroom hadn't worked in years. It really was a disaster.

"The house has to be cleaned up and some things should be removed. You might even think of having a house sale." I could tell he was not interested in this suggestion. His brother lived in Arizona and wouldn't be a part of something like that. "There are people who will price everything and keep a percentage of the sales for their fee." He showed no interest in my suggestion. "If there is less furniture in a room it will look larger."

"Let's put it on the market just as it is and see what happens."

The overpriced listing contract was signed at the price they wanted. I had several open house Sundays at the property site but I could not find an interested buyer. I mailed my property for sale information to the residents in the area, but still no one was interested.

The seller was in touch with me every week. What can I tell an owner if a property does not sell? "We are in a depressed market; it doesn't show well." The only other thing to say is, "Reduce the price." But the owner never wants to hear this. The heirs want to hear it even less. I can never understand this. They are receiving a gift yet they want more. I've seen them hold out for a few thousand dollars. In six months after paying heat, taxes, and insurance sometimes they end up with less than the original offer.

One afternoon at an open house I was surprised to have one of the town attorneys come to look. I didn't know he was looking for a new location. Immediately he could see the possibility of this being his new office.

In this town the ordinance states that if you have an office in a residential area, you must reside in the property. I knew where he lived, because I sold him the house. His office was located in a business area in a colonial office building.

I love to sell real estate and make my commission, but I didn't like to get involved in a sale that is contingent on a variance. There can be all sorts of delays by the attorneys and the town.

Sometimes it is necessary to notify owners in the area so they can object if they feel it will affect them unfairly. Months can go by before a decision is reached. I like a nice clean sale. Go to the closing and pick up the commission check.

I wondered if I should question him about this. He's an attorney. He knows the laws of the town. Sometimes it is better not to say too much. I happen to know how variances can tie up the sale of a property but I have a responsibility to my seller to know all the facts. "Are you planning to live here?" I knew he had three sons and a wife.

"Yes, I'll be living upstairs."

That was either a lie or he was going to be separated from his family. I had to take him at his word.

"I am interested in this property, but I have been looking out of town. I found something I like, but we have not been able to arrive at an agreeable price."

While he was talking I was thinking, "I guess this is going nowhere." I had high hopes since he seemed so interested. He even had his wife over to look at the house. We talked a little longer. He envisioned the living room as the reception area, the dining room as the conference room, one bedroom as his office, and the other bedroom for his secretary. He seemed so interested that I hoped the sale of the out-of-town property did not materialize.

After the open house I spoke to Paul. I explained what had happened, but I didn't want to make it sound too optimistic. He told me his brother would be in town in a day or two. I was hopeful I could get the brother to act on having the house cleaned out.

I never did get to see him but I guess the condition of the house must have bothered him. A short time went by and when I showed the property it was in much better condition.

I kept in touch with the attorney and little by little his interest in the other property seemed to dissolve. It was quite a distance from our town, in another county. He would be leaving all his clients. It would have the same effect as starting his practice all over again. Finally he told me he hoped to buy the out-of-town property and hold on to it until his retirement. This did not seem feasible, since he needed a new location for his office now. There were some internal problems he did not confide to me.

"I'm ready to make an offer on this property. Why don't we meet at the house to take care of that?" I was pleased to hear this. The phone calls had been ongoing for three weeks. "Tomorrow is Saturday. I can be there at eleven o'clock. How is that for you?"

"Eleven is good. I'll bring some contracts and we can get started." I stopped at my office to make a few calls and check on my listings. There were no emergencies. I decided I might as well fill in the contract, except for the price, down payment, and the mortgage amount. As soon as I sat down to type, the office chatter started. You have a contract? What property is it on? Who's listing is it? I hated all this. They all knew it was none of their business, but everyone was hoping the contract was on a listing of theirs. I didn't like this because if someone had an interested buyer they might call that person. They might tell them, "If you are interested in that property hurry and make an offer." Of course this is not ethical but one never knows how a salesperson will operate in a slow market. I removed the contract from the typewriter and decided I would type it at home. I had all the information in my briefcase.

The next morning at eleven we were at the house. His wife also was there and he wanted to make another tour of the house and basement. He had some questions about removing the old refrigerator and the personal effects of the owner. I added this to the contract along with a closing date.

"And what are you offering?"

The Psychology of Selling Real Estate 35

"I've checked out all the recent, closed sales and we will be offering $160,000." I looked at him. I think my mouth was open. It was the same amount I originally said it would sell for!

"I'll put that in the contract and we will see what the brothers have to say." He was paying cash, so there was no mortgage contingency. After the contracts were signed they decided to look upstairs again. I wondered if Paul would remember this was the price I told him it would sell for? Would they accept it? If not, will the buyer raise the price? These are the same old questions that come up at every sale. While they were upstairs I called Paul.

"Hello, I have an offer for you. Will you be home for the next hour or so?"

"How much is it for?" A logical question but one I never discussed on the phone.

"Let's talk about it when I get there. Half hour okay?"

"We'll be here."

After they left, I locked up the house and drove over to Paul's office. They were happy to see me and were in a good mood.

"I knew he was interested. I saw him stop at the house and look at it the other day when I was inside. Where's the contract?"

Paul and I have known each other since grammar school, so we are a little informal. Before I show it to him should I say, "Remember what I told you about the price?" Or maybe I better not. I opened the folder and gave one to him and his wife.

"He took twenty thousand dollars off the price! I'm not interested in this."

"Before you turn it down let me point out, there is no mortgage contingency to hold things up. It can be a quick closing. There is no clause for an office variance, which can delay a closing sometimes for months." He looked at his wife but there was no communication. He was shaking his head no.

"Why not give your brother a call and talk this over."

"He said he wanted me to call if there was an offer. I am in charge of the estate but we will have to agree."

I realize it is very difficult to be in charge of an estate. If it is a family situation then it becomes more difficult. And if the people involved but not in charge reside out of state, then it becomes extremely difficult. The opportunity to discuss small issues is not available. Then when there are a number of small issues it seems overwhelming.

I did not hear from Paul on Sunday. On Monday afternoon the attorney called. "I am curious, have you heard anything?"

"I presented the offer and he was surprised that you had taken twenty thousand dollars off the asking price."

"LuLu, I know what the nearby houses have sold for. I've even looked at a few of them."

"He will be talking with his brother and as soon as he has a counteroffer I'm sure he will be back to us." I really had nothing else to say until that time.

Waiting for the response to an offer or a counteroffer is the time when nervous tension starts to build. Your mind begins to play games; will they counter, will it be too high for me, am I doing the right thing, will someone else come in with a better offer.... Finally, when you are very anxious you wonder if you should have gone higher in the first place. And of course the monthly charges begin to rear their ugly heads. Now you wonder if you can afford the house in the first place.

"I think I would like to take another look at the house."

"Are you having second thoughts about purchasing the property?"

"No. I want to take another look at how I thought the layout of offices could be arranged."

At least he didn't say he wanted to withdraw his offer. It is very difficult to second-guess buyers and sellers.

The Psychology of Selling Real Estate

"I was planning to call Paul later in the day. I will call you as soon as I have any information. Then if you like we can go over to the house again." This seemed to satisfy him.

I had a few houses I wanted to ride by so I left the office. While I was out I passed Paul's property and saw his car in the driveway. I decided to stop and have a talk with him. As I walked up to the house he came out of the side door.

"Hi, Paul. I'm glad you're here." We were standing in the driveway.

"I came over to look at the house as if I were a buyer."

"That's an excellent idea. Look at the driveway down there where the roots of the tree have raised it up." He turned and looked and shook his head.

"I had a talk with my brother last night and he said we should not think of this as being our mother's home. We should think as if we were the buyers, and what we would want to do to the house."

"I think that's an excellent way to go. Sentiment often colors our thinking."

"I'm going to get back to my brother this evening, then I'll call you."

I left to finish what I had started. When I arrived at the office I called the attorney. I explained what had occurred and told him I would get a call after the brothers spoke that evening. He seemed satisfied with this and decided to make another inspection after we heard from Paul.

About nine o'clock Paul called. "We've decided that $170,000 is our price. We think it is fair. What do you think?"

He really doesn't want to hear what I'm thinking because it will be, "That's the price I told you to list the property at to begin with." Instead I said, "I think that's a good place to be." He mentioned a few reasons for the price they came up with. At this point I was only interested in what the buyers were going to say. I assured him I would talk to the buyers and tell them the counteroffer.

As the realtor, the person in the middle, I called the buyer. "I just had a call from Paul and he is countering with $170,000." Normally, I would handle this differently but, being an attorney, he is very familiar with the process. As I suspected he had his answer ready.

"One hundred and sixty-five; this is my final offer." There was a pause, "The house needs a lot of work and I am not pressed to move immediately. Please tell them that."

I knew he meant what he said by the tone of his voice. As the person in the middle it is difficult to keep everyone happy. "I think it is a good offer. I will call him now but I doubt if he will have an answer tonight."

"Don't hesitate to call me if you have good news."

Do I start by telling Paul, "This is the final offer," or do I tell him the price first and let him get excited and tell me that $170,000 is what they want? Then I can tell him, "This is the final offer." I think I must take into account that I know Paul's personality. He loves to talk, loves to be right, and he is a salesperson.

"Hi, Paul. I hope it's not too late to call."

"Not at all. I hoped you would."

"The buyer has put a lot of thought into this purchase. He is not being pushed out of his office. There is no rush." I paused to let this sink in. "This is his final offer, $165,000."

"What do you mean *final?*" I heard irritation in his voice.

Calmly, with much emphasis, I said, "He is not going up any higher."

"We came down from $180,000!" His voice reflected anger.

Now I guess I have to tell him what I told him two months ago. "Do you remember when I listed this property I told you, 'It will probably sell for $165,000?' He knows the value of the surrounding properties."

"I think it's worth $170,000." I know Paul loves to be right.

"Paul, how many other offers have you had in two months?"

There was a pause. He hated to say it, "None."

"I know how you feel. But this is his best offer and the only one you have." He was silent. I heard a long sigh. "I think you better have another talk with your brother. The two of you better give this very serious consideration." I said this very slowly to give it a sound of finality.

It was half past ten before we finished talking. I was exhausted. I was tired of being cautious of what I would or could say. Anyone who thinks selling real estate is easy and a fast way to make money is wrong! You have to try a lot of psychology and sometimes even that does not work.

It was too late to call the attorney. I decided a glass of wine and my soft snuggly robe would feel good while I listened to the late night news.

The next morning before I left for the office I called the attorney. He understood that we would have to wait until the evening for the two brothers to make a decision. Once again he reminded me that his offer was firm.

Very unexpectedly in the afternoon Paul called. He was able to reach his brother early in the day and had made some phone calls about emptying the contents of the house.

"It's going to cost about two thousand dollars to have the house emptied and cleaned up. We would like to cover this with $167,000. We would be happy with that."

I guess they each wanted $85,000. I noticed how reluctant he was to say they were accepting the offer and would like to cover additional costs. I was happy a decision had been made.

"Paul, I will call the buyer right now. I hope he will agree. I'll get back to you as soon as I have an answer."

I decided to drive over to the law office. He was just finishing a closing so I waited.

"Come on in LuLu." He indicated a chair and I sat down. "What's the good news?"

Very firmly I said, "We are going to finalize this today. We are very close." I explained about the two thousand dollars for the cleanup.

He reached for the phone and dialed a number. While it rang he said to me, "My cousin works for the Diocese of Newark, helping the immigrants and displaced families; you know fires and such." He stopped talking to me.

"Hello Joe. How are things going?" He waited to hear the answer. "A big fire? Really? I might be able to help you out. I have a whole house full of furniture and clothing that you can have." His cousin was talking. "Hold on a minute."

He told me there had been a big fire and Joe needed furniture and household items for the displaced families. Joe had a crew of men who would come and remove whatever was not wanted.

"What a great connection to have! This is wonderful. I'll get back to Paul and we can zero in on the closing date."

He said to his cousin, "I'll let you know what day to send the truck," and hung up.

I started to leave when he said, "Call Paul from here and we can settle this now."

"Great idea." He dialed the number and handed me the phone.

"Paul your problems are all solved. The buyer will empty the entire house, after you decide what you want to keep. No expense to you at all. One hundred and sixty-five thousand dollars is the final offer."

"But, I don't understand. He will pay to empty the house?" Again his inability to just accept was rearing its head.

"It shouldn't make any difference to you how he goes about this. It just means you aren't responsible for paying to clean out the house." He wanted to know every detail even if it did not concern him. I finally said with a little irritation in my voice, "Do you want the $165,000 or not?" The attorney looked at me with raised eyebrows.

The Psychology of Selling Real Estate

Very quickly, with emphasis I heard, "Yes, I'll take it!"

"Good. I'll stop at your office in a half hour." He said he would be waiting.

The attorney said, "I got a little concerned when you said, 'Do you want the $165,000 or not?'"

"I just had to shake him up a little."

"You've done a good job. Thank you. I know this will work out just great for me." I had him initial the changes in the contract, then I left.

A short while later I was at Paul's. "Now I will tell you all the details." I finished and he had more questions. Finally, I said, "All your mother's possessions are going to help make a few families very happy."

"I'm happy about that. She loved her furniture. We had many happy dinners around her dining room table. Maybe someone else will too." He initialed the changes in the contract.

The closing date was set for the middle of November. Everyone was pleased. Joe even sent his cousin a letter from the diocese saying how pleased they were to receive the contents of the house for the displaced families.

At the closing I said, "Hopefully, families will enjoy Thanksgiving and Christmas with your mother's possessions."

Paul said, "Maybe Thanksgiving and Hanukkah."

CHAPTER 7

The Cat and Mouse Game

What motivates someone to respond to an advertisement? Some words have magic and some fall short of developing an image. In the real estate business the objective is to make the phones ring. I guess the words "A Charming Victorian" caught this reader's eye.

"Opportunity Realtors, may I help you?"

"Yes, you have a house advertised in the paper that reads 'A Charming Victorian.' What can you tell me about it?"

The art of talking to a prospective buyer is not to tell them everything they want to know until you have the information needed to build a relationship.

"I'll be happy to give you the information. It's on a very nice quiet street. Are you familiar with the town?"

"Oh yes, we don't live too far from there."

"Why are you moving?"

"Oh it's not for me. It's for my daughter. She works in New York City and doesn't have time to follow up on the houses that are for sale."

"Well, this is an older house with a nice kitchen. The living and dining rooms are average size. The three bedrooms on the second floor are not overly large but the master bedroom is on the third floor and is very large. Do you think she might be interested in something like this?"

"I'll have to drive by to take a look. What is the address?"

Now I have to get my information or the price of the advertisement is wasted. It's important how I do this. "In case this is not what your daughter might like, I will be happy to call you with new listings as they come on the market. Please give me your name and phone number."

She was very accommodating and said, "I'm Mrs. Gill, and my number is 555-1212. What is the address and the price? I'd like to drive by this weekend."

I gave her what she wanted after I had a little insight into why her daughter needed help and where I could reach the mother. Many times parents call when they are trying to convince their children to buy property, but the children have no such intention. Perhaps her daughter is ready to move and the mother is trying to be helpful. Most of the time parents and children don't agree on the location or the style of a home. The biggest disagreement is usually on the price of the property. I didn't put too much hope in this call.

My telephone time at the office was over. I went to look at properties that had just come on the market that morning. This is the only way I will really know what is for sale. As yet I don't know exactly what Mrs. Gill's daughter wants. But when I find out, if I have seen it, a bell will go off. It's like a jigsaw puzzle. You have to put all the pieces together in the right places. This is the secret of sales! That's what I love about real estate, knowing what house goes with what buyer.

Monday morning rolled around and I decided to call Mrs. Gill to see if she was really sincere and had driven past the house. "Good morning this is LuLu from Opportunity Realty. How are you today?"

"I'm fine, thank you."

No recognition, very disinterested. For all I know she might have called a dozen realtors last week. This does not sound too great. I better add a little excitement to this conversation.

"You called my office about a house for your daughter who works in New York. I gave you the address of a property in Nutley. Do you think she might have any interest in that house?"

"Oh no, that's too old. She's looking for a contemporary house."

"A contemporary house!" I was so excited. If this mother really knows what her daughter wants, I had just the house for her. "I have the perfect house for her. It's not in the same town. It's in Bloomfield."

"Bloomfield! That's where I live. Where in Bloomfield is it?" The excitement in her voice told me she would love to have her daughter live close to her.

"It's on Main Street near St. Mark's Church."

"I live two block from there! When can I see the house?"

Just from the tone of her voice I could tell she was ready to look at the house immediately.

"I'll call the homeowner to see if someone is there. I will get right back to you."

The owner was not in. We were the listing broker and had the key. I called Mrs. O'Brien at her office to tell her I would be showing her home. Then I called Mrs. Gill back.

"We can see the house anytime you want. We have a key and everyone is at work."

"How about right now?" I wished all my callers were this excited.

"I'll meet you at 999 Main Street in fifteen minutes." Boy, she was really anxious to have her baby near her!

This was a truly nice house. The O'Briens had obtained it in an unusual way. That is another story within a story. Once Richard O'Brien became the owner he enlarged and modernized it to his family's needs. He was very talented and did a great job on the renovations. His wife had decorated the den, three bedrooms, and three bathrooms to perfection. They installed central air conditioning and designed a large modern gourmet kitchen. The master bedroom was king-sized with walk-in closets that had adjustable shelves, shoe racks, and mirrored doors. The laundry room was on the second floor. This is unusual, but as any woman will tell you,

The Cat and Mouse Game 45

this is the perfect location. After all, that's where the laundry comes from and where it goes back to.

Mrs. Gill and I arrived at the same time. "Good morning. I live just down the block and this is wonderfully convenient." She was very excited, even before she inspected the interior.

"I'm glad you like the location. Wait until you see the inside. You will love it."

I unlocked the door and we went in. There was a large piece of paper mache artwork in the living room. It was a man's body in a sitting position. Sitting on nothing; I mean literally sitting on nothing.

When she saw it she said, "Oh my son-in-law will love this! He's an artist." As we went toward the kitchen she turned back. "The living room is a good size." When we got to the kitchen she stopped. "What a gorgeous kitchen!"

"The owner is a gourmet cook. It is laid out very well with ample counter space and lovely cabinets," I said. I told her again that there was central air conditioning.

"That's wonderful. I wish I had it in my home."

We inspected the den and then went to the second floor. The master bedroom was magnificent, huge with skylights and several windows, a dressing area, and a private bath.

"My daughter will love this. Can you show it to her tonight? Her husband will be working late because they are supposed to go on vacation tomorrow."

"I'll be happy to show it tonight, but if they are going on vacation tomorrow how can anything be decided?"

"I know she will love this. She can make a decision very quickly if necessary."

I got the impression that her daughter was in control. The mother loved everything about the house, even the bus at the front door that went to New York City where her daughter and son-in-law worked.

That evening when mother, father, and daughter arrived, the O'Briens were out to dinner. The daughter was young, about twenty-four, highly made up, and very energetic. As soon as we stepped into the house Loretta took over the tour. Was she ever in control! She had an air of self-confidence, bordering on arrogance, going from room to room noticing every feature, not hesitating to give approval to all the nice details. I was beginning to get a little excited. Maybe she will be able to convince her husband that he must like it too.

"We are supposed to go on vacation tomorrow, but I want Louis to see this house before we leave. Make arrangements to show it at half past eight tomorrow morning."

She did not ask if I was available, or if it was too early for the owners, just to do it! I had to remind myself to be helpful and yet not seem too anxious. I do have to make a living and the commission on a sale is what does it.

"I will have to get in touch with the owners to see how that time fits into their schedule. It will be Saturday and the children will be home from school. But I'll try for half past eight."

"I'll be at my mother's. You can call me there. I think you have the number."

With that they walked out the door to the front of the house while I locked up. She strutted up the sidewalk, looking at the roof, trying to give the impression she knew what she was supposed to look for.

As I started my car I said, "I'll call you later about tomorrow." There was something about this woman that I did not care for. Back at the office, I called Mrs. O'Brien and left a message on her recorder. I told her that my buyer would like to come back in the morning, at half past eight to show her husband the property.

Later when Mrs. O'Brien called she said, "That's no problem. We're up early. The kids will be up too. That's fine. Did they like it?"

"The mother, father, and daughter loved it. Loretta was anxious for her husband to see it in the morning."

The Cat and Mouse Game

The property had been on the market for a few months. Since the O'Briens knew where they were moving, they were eager to find a buyer. They bought this house about eight years ago because they wanted to live next door to Richard's mother who was developing Parkinson's. Recently the mother died. They were going to move in with his father, since he needed someone to care for him.

The next day I arrived at the property before Loretta and Louis. The owners were waiting for me. The children were walking out the rear door to the grandfather's house. The O'Briens were asking about the prospective buyers when the doorbell rang. They sat down to have a cup of coffee, while I answered the door. It's a smart owner who knows how to stay out of the way.

I was just able to say hello to the husband before Loretta took over. She directed him to each room and pointed out all the amenities that I had talked about the night before. Louis was low-keyed, quiet, and dressed very casually. He was about the same height as Loretta. I just trailed along. After all, if she wanted to sell the house for me why should I object? It was obvious that she was very excited about the property. Louis listened to everything she was saying, nodding in agreement. I decided to leave them alone in the master bedroom.

After a while they came downstairs holding hands and smiling. We next inspected the basement, then spent some time with the owners hearing about the new central air system and the expensive additions they had built-in to the house. After many questions were answered we left.

Outside Loretta said, "We are leaving at two this afternoon for Puerto Rico. We like the house but cannot make a decision so quickly. We will be gone for only three days."

There was no way I could draw up a contract and negotiate a price in such a short time. So I had to let them go. Chances of another broker coming up with a buyer were very slight since we were in a slow market.

"When you get back in town call me. Let me know what your plans are at that time." I tried to act casual even though I knew they loved it, and I wanted to put a contract together immediately.

"You don't think someone will come along and make an offer, do you?" Loretta was doing all the talking.

"I have no way of knowing. But if you feel that you will make an offer when you return, I can indicate that to the owners."

She was very excited and said, "Great! That way the owners will hold off taking an offer, should one come along. That's good. Tell them that."

I said, "Have a good time on the weekend," and turned to go inside.

She called out, "Don't show it to anyone else while we are gone." I explained that I could not stop anyone from looking at the property.

Inside the house the owner said, "Well what's the story, are they interested?" Their body language was so strong; any novice could tell that Loretta and Louis were definitely interested.

"It's the first house I have showed to them. It is unfortunate that they are going on vacation, because I think they would be ready to make an offer. With the tight time schedule it's impossible for them to do it now."

The owners were excited that they had someone who was interested. The O'Briens are not new at the cat and mouse game of real estate negotiating. This was the second house they were selling. He said, "They will only be gone for a long weekend, so we will be patient." This couple worked beautifully together. Neither one ever said or indicated more than they wanted anyone to know.

"You're right, it will only be a few days before they make an offer. Since you have waited this long you can be patient a little longer."

I wanted them to realize I knew the property had been for sale without a realtor for a few months. It was on a busy street,

The Cat and Mouse Game 49

but it was also convenient for anyone who needs the New York City bus, which was what Loretta and Louis wanted. Since I was involved with other buyers, the weekend went by very quickly. On Tuesday I received a call from Loretta. I knew it would not be Louis calling. She told me about the great weather they had in Puerto Rico. Her voice was very firm, not feminine at all when she said, "We like the house and want to make an offer."

"Good I'm glad you're ready because the longer you wait the greater the chance is that someone else will look at the property. When can you both meet me at my office?"

"We'll have dinner at my mother's. We can be with you by half past seven. Will you have information for us about mortgage rates?"

"If you can be at my office at that time, I will arrange for the financial service representative to be there also." Our office has an in-house financial service representative, which makes it very convenient for us to qualify our buyers. It is also advantageous to the buyer. They will know how much mortgage they can carry. At this time they also find out what down payment will be required of them. When the buyer has been qualified, the homeowner can feel a certain amount of assurance that the buyer will be able to obtain a mortgage. That is, if the buyer is truthful and tells the representative all the financial facts.

That evening, this very assertive, aggressive woman came with her very determined father and they brought the quiet, unassuming husband. They talked about the house, but now it was not about the wonderful amenities. It was about all the negatives, a busy street, a small yard, and only a one-car garage.

"How do you think they will feel about an offer of $175,000?" Mr. Gill asked.

My job is very difficult; I'm the middle person. I try to make all people happy. The buyer wants to buy for the lowest price and the seller wants to sell for the highest price. "I think they will be very happy to hear Loretta and Louis like their home enough to make an offer. Will they take it? I don't know. After all, the asking price is thirty thousand dollars higher."

"Oh come on," Loretta said, "you know what they will take."

Her husband just looked from her to her father and back again, but the truth was, the owners were very savvy people; they never revealed their hand to me.

I explained to Loretta, "What the O'Briens will, or will not, take was never confided to me." I also suggested that they make an offer close to what they hope to pay for the property. Otherwise we might be insulting the seller or getting into a tug of war.

The father said, "I think it's a fair offer, so let's start there." I guess Loretta's determined character came from him.

Loretta said, "Put a contract together for that price and let's see what they say. Now can we talk about a mortgage?"

As I went to prepare the contract I told them the financial service representative would be right in.

I wish I had the opportunity to acquaint Ms. Silver with the personalities she was about to deal with. I knew she was experienced and I assumed capable of working with various temperaments. I left it in her hands. The financial interview took about forty-five minutes. It was necessary for me to interrupt once. I could see that the father and daughter were putting Ms. Silver through the wringer. She informed them of the rates and explained how many points the banks and mortgage brokers were quoting. After much interrogation Loretta informed the representative that they had already spoken to a "friend" and a bank or two. It then became apparent what they were doing to the representative. They were comparing her rates, points, and terms. This is smart to do, but the attitude that Loretta projected was wrong. In the end she came up with a challenge. She wanted the best rate and the points shaved. When I returned with the contract ready for their signatures, I heard Loretta say, "Let us know if you can meet those terms."

The Cat and Mouse Game

The fiancial service representative said, "I'll make a few calls and get in touch with you tomorrow."

Her voice was not quite as effervescent as when she had come into the room to meet them. I guess she sensed that the time spent with Louis and Loretta would not generate a mortgage application.

"Let's go over the contract and get your signatures. I would like to contact the O'Briens and try to meet with them this evening." The basic contract did not raise any questions but when it came to the inclusions, she wanted everything! And everything she wanted, I had to include. As we got to the end of the contract I asked if they had an attorney. Daughter and father looked at each other and didn't come up with an answer.

"Do you have a suggestion?" Loretta asked.

As I always tell my buyers, "It's best to use a local attorney and someone who has a good background in real estate transactions. I can give you a list of a few attorneys." They seemed satisfied with this.

We all got up to leave when Loretta said, "As soon as you speak to the O'Briens and have an answer, call us."

By now the time was quarter to ten. I had a full day, but real estate rules are hard and fast: "the offer must be presented expeditiously." The rules also say I must contact the listing sales associate about the offer. I called Mrs. O'Brien but she wanted to wait until the next day, since her husband was out of town.

At ten o'clock I called Mrs. Gill's home and Loretta answered the phone. "I'm afraid you will have to wait until tomorrow." Before I could finish the sentence, she interrupted.

"What are they waiting for? I want an answer tonight!"

"Loretta, you didn't give me a chance to finish. We have to wait because Mr. O'Brien is out of town. He will be back tomorrow." I could feel my resentment building up against Loretta.

"All right, call me first thing in the morning." She sounded very arrogant.

"I don't know what time he will be in, but I will call you as soon as I have something to tell you." I wasn't about to call her until I knew when I would meet with the O'Briens.

"I'll call you before I go to lunch. Good-bye."

In over twenty years I have come across many different personalities while selling real estate. I have never met a female who was so dictatorial and arrogant. The following day I was out of the office for a good part of the morning previewing the new listings. Back at the office, after lunch, I had several calls waiting to be answered. One was from Loretta. I had a few attorneys to contact, but there was nothing from the O'Briens. I called Mrs. O'Brien at work and she said Richard had called to say he would be in about half past five if the traffic was not too bad. "Richard will call you when he gets in." In all the confusion I had forgotten to call the listing agent. A big "no, no" in this business. I got on the phone and called Martha.

"Hi, I have good news. There's an offer on your listing on Main Street."

"Great, is it a good one?"

"It's a beginning."

"Mr. O'Brien is out of town," Martha said.

"I know. He'll be home about half past five. They'll call and let me know what time will be good for them to see me."

Now comes the waiting game. Selling real estate is very intriguing. I love the waiting and trying to figure out what the next move will be for either the buyer or the seller. Will they be anxious or disinterested? Will they jump at the first offer? It has happened. Will the buyer expect a bargain and throw in a low-ball offer? Will they ever go high enough to satisfy the seller? A low offer can be insulting. What will happen between this knowledgeable owner and this aggressive buyer?

"Hello Loretta, I just heard that Richard would be home around half past five."

"I tried to reach you earlier, but you weren't in." Her voice told me she was impatient with me.

The Cat and Mouse Game

"I know, I was out on business, at an attorney's office and previewing new properties." I wanted her to know that I had other clients. "When Richard gets home he will call. Then I will go over to present your offer. As soon as I have something to tell you, I will be in touch with you."

"It's a very strained feeling not being able to get an answer right away," Loretta said.

When you are a control person I guess it is difficult. "I can understand how you feel, but these situations do occur. We have no control of Richard's time." I tried to settle her down. "Just as soon as I have a response from the O'Briens, I will contact you."

"I'll be at my mother's; you can call me there." That was the end of the conversation.

I was still at the office at half past five when Martha called to say that Richard was home and I could go over as soon as I was ready. Even though Martha is a member of my office she represents the owner and I represent the buyer. We each have our own clients. When I arrived the three of them were in the kitchen talking.

"I could tell they liked the house," Mrs. O'Brien said. "Have they made a good offer?"

Richard rushed to say, "Because we have put a lot of money into this house."

"I know it was obvious that they liked it. The Rodriquez's have made what they think is a fair offer." I opened my briefcase and handed each of them a copy of the contract. Everyone's eyes immediately went to the price.

"It's much too low," Richard said and put the papers down. I waited to hear something more while Martha continued to search out the other details.

She asked, "Do you mind stepping into the living room for a few minutes while we talk?"

"Of course not." I got up and walked out of the room. I knew Martha would point out to the O'Briens that the buyers

were putting down 30 percent which would make it easy to obtain a mortgage; also that the closing date would please them.

After a short while Martha said, "LuLu, come on back. We have a few things to discuss." I felt they might be ready to do a little negotiating. "We've talked about the down payment and the closing, but the items they want included for the price they are offering is not possible."

Richard continued, "The six-burner restaurant stove cost over six thousand dollars and the refrigerator-freezer was five thousand dollars. As the listing states, we are not including them. The stove will be replaced." I could see the three of them were in agreement.

The Cat and Mouse Game

"I will tell the buyers your decision on the appliances, but what about the price? Do you have a counteroffer?"

Without hesitation Richard said, "It's not acceptable. We are thirty thousand dollars apart. Tell them to come closer to the listed price."

"LuLu, you know what's out there for $175,000." I knew she was right. Martha started to get up.

"I will talk to them. I'm sure I'll be back. Thanks for your time." I walked to the door with Martha but she stayed on to talk with the owners.

I got in the car and started for the office but realized I had not had dinner yet. Instead of going to the office I drove home. In my mind I was going over all the events that had led up to the offer. How will I handle the next step? I think this will be a long walk to the finish line. Richard can be as hard-nosed as Loretta tries to be. But I know she wants this house very badly. I'm not going to pull any punches with her. I'm going to be just as abrupt as she is and leave everything in her court.

The phone was ringing as I unlocked the door. "I hope it's not Loretta," I thought. But before I reached for it the ringing stopped. I was so hungry. I was going to call Loretta after I ate. Twenty minutes later the phone rang again. Thank goodness for microwave ovens. I had finished eating and was ready for an anxious buyer. "Hello?"

"Oh you're home." Never did I hear a polite hello.

"Yes, I just got in a short time ago and was about to call you."

"Well, what did they say? Did you tell them we thought the offer was fair?" I knew from the excitement in her voice that she was uptight.

"As soon as I presented the offer, they rejected it." Before I could continue she started.

"Do they realize that $175,000 is a lot of money for a house in Bloomfield? My mother and father are two blocks away and they will never get that much for their home." I could hear a man's muffled voice in the background. "What was their counteroffer?" I guessed her father was instructing her on what to say.

"Loretta, they would not make a counteroffer. I think they were insulted by the thirty-thousand-dollar reduction you took on the asking price." I could hear more background talking.

"Just a minute, I want to talk to my father." His voice was low and calm. She came back with, "What did they say about the appliances?"

"The stove is to be replaced and the refrigerator is not included. I believe I explained that to you on our first visit to the house."

"I know, I know, but I thought we could get it. We're going to do some talking. I'll get back to you later." She hung up.

It was about half past seven when I sat down at the computer to pull up some comparable listings and home sales when the phone rang. It was the financial service representative. "I just had a call from your buyer, Loretta. She is trying to get me to give her a mortgage for a half point less than a friend has quoted to her. Not only that, but she wants me to, as she put it, 'shave a point off the origination fee.'"

I laughed, "She is a piece of work."

"How close are you to making this sale?"

"We aren't close at all. They took thirty thousand dollars off the asking price." I filled her in with what happened at the O'Brien's. "Loretta told me that the boyfriend of someone at her office just started working at a mortgage brokerage company. I guess he promised her a good deal."

"I don't know how he can follow through on the rate and points she said he quoted to her. In fact I know he can't." She sounded exasperated.

"I know you always do the best you can and if you can't meet it, just move on to your next client. Who knows if she is telling the truth about the points and rate." Sometimes a buyer will exaggerate a little about what has been offered to

The Cat and Mouse Game

them. "She's trying to save money so she can go up on the offered price. I'm sure mamma and daddy will come up with some money." I thanked her for the effort she had made.

"I better hang up." I heard her take a deep breath, "I promised Loretta I would call her back. First I wanted to find out if this was ready to go forward, before I made a call to my supervisor to see if there was something we could do. She has a very good rate from her friend. She should take it."

A short while later Loretta was back on the phone to me. "This is the very best we will do. We are going up twenty thousand dollars and they must leave the stove and refrigerator."

I have learned so much psychology since I started selling real estate. I wanted to say, "What do you mean 'must!'" I have learned to control myself.

"I'm sure they will be pleased to hear the new price," I said very calmly. "I'll be happy to change the price on the contract and present it to them. It's half past eight. When can you meet me at my office?"

With a huge sigh she said very forcefully, "I haven't had dinner yet. Just call them and tell them what I said!"

"I'm sorry, that is against the rules of the board of realtors. No verbal offers."

"They know us! We signed one contract!" Her voice was a pitch higher.

"I'm sorry." I said softly.

"This isn't fair!"

I could tell she was getting very frustrated. "Loretta," I said very slowly, "since I practically have to pass your mother's house to get to the O'Briens, I'll be glad to stop at your mother's to get your signatures."

"That's where we are, that will work. See you in a little while." She didn't even acknowledge the concession I was making.

As I started my car I remembered one of the first sales I tried to put together. A neighbor's house was for sale. It needed to be updated. I called a local builder who specialized in buying and renovating. He and his wife looked at the property late in the evening and liked it. After inspecting the interior and exterior of the house he made a verbal offer. I suggested we go to my office to draw up a contract and he said, "LuLu, give him our price and tell him we'll sign the contract tomorrow." I went back in and gave them the news. They were happy with the offer and said they would see me the next day.

In the morning when the buyers came to my office they decided to offer less money for the property. I was flabbergasted! This was very embarrassing. When I presented the lesser offer to the sellers they were vehemently angry. They hollered at me and said they believed I had lied to them the night before. I was humiliated. I have never taken another verbal offer.

I had no trouble finding the Gill's house. The contracts were changed and initialed. The father said, "I hope you will be able to convince them to take this offer. I don't think there is another house in the area that is this expensive."

"I agree with you. But there is not another house in the area that has the square footage or the modern amenities that this one has."

He shook his head ever so slightly and said, "But she likes this one."

"She has good taste. Let's see how they like this offer." I smiled and said, "I'll do the very best I can. I think it's a good offer." I asked to use their phone and called Martha to tell her we had a better offer. It was nine o'clock and she wasn't too happy with the thought that she might have to go out again this evening. I told her I was only a few blocks from the O'Briens.

She said, "Let me call them and see what they want to do."

While standing near the phone Loretta, father, and mother all were telling me their version of what I must tell the sellers.

The Cat and Mouse Game 59

I didn't have a chance to say very much. When the phone rang, I was happy to pick it up. Martha said, "LuLu, I've had a busy day. I really don't feel like going out at this time."

My day hadn't exactly been relaxing either. "What do you want to do?" In the real estate world the listing broker is in control, but there is always a way to urge them into action. "I'm here at Loretta's parents' home and they are anxious to have the new offer presented tonight." Now Martha knew the buyers were aware of her reluctance to present the new offer.

She hesitated a moment, "All right, give me twenty minutes. I'll call the O'Briens again and tell them to expect us."

"I'll meet you there in a few minutes." I wanted to leave the house as fast as I could. I couldn't take any more instructions. I parked in front of the O'Briens and opened the windows to let in the cool air. I wanted to think. We are just ten thousand dollars off the asking price. No one ever expects to get the full price. Can the buyers come up a little more if necessary? If the O'Briens want more money what can I bargain with? I'll come up with something. A car pulled up behind me. It was Martha and it was a quarter after nine.

"You better have a good offer to get me out at this time of night." Buyers are not the only ones who can be arrogant.

I told her, "The best offers come in late at night, when everyone's resistance is low."

The O'Briens opened the door. They appeared very happy to see me. I felt the offer was great and they should accept it, but who knows what is in the mind of your opponent. They were my opponents because they were pushing to get the most they could and my buyers were hoping to give the least they would have to give.

We had some pleasant talk and ended up at the kitchen table. When we were all settled I took out the new contract. "I know you have done some wonderful things with this house. It's been done in good taste and my clients love it. But, there is only so far they can go and still be able to afford this house." I handed a contract to each of them and sat back in the chair. The stove and refrigerator were still included. I saw that they were reading more than just the price. "I think it's a very good offer. It's the first house in this town to ever sell for this much money."

"I really wanted to get two hundred thousand dollars, and I would leave the refrigerator," Richard said again.

"I doubt if I can get it. Let me call them and see what we can do to close this transaction. I'll use the phone in the den." He is really a tough seller. As I dialed the number I knew Loretta would answer.

"Yes?"

"Loretta, They like your offer, but . . ."

"But what?" She interrupted with emphasis.

"Try to stay calm. He really wanted to get two hund . . ."

"No way!"

"Wait a minute! He really wanted to get two hundred thousand dollars and leave only the refrigerator. Do you think you could come up with three thousand dollars and I will tell him it is the last offer for everything? This would include both the stove and the refrigerator. The price would be one hundred and ninety-eight thousand dollars." I took a deep breath, "You would get both appliances but he would not get his two hundred thousand."

"Just a minute." I could hear a lot of muffled talk.

Martha stuck her head in the room. "Any news?" Now they were the anxious ones.

"Not yet," I answered.

A few minutes later Loretta was back, "Tell them I will give them two thousand dollars more. That's $197,000, and that is it! Either they take it or we walk."

"Loretta, if they don't take it they are out of their minds. I'll get back to you very shortly."

I walked into the kitchen and without even sitting down I said, "One hundred and ninety-seven thousand dollars, take

The Cat and Mouse Game   61

it or leave it!" I started to pick up my portfolio and at the same time reached for the contracts and looked Richard straight in his eyes.

His wife looked at him and said, "Richard . . ."

He said, "I really wanted two hundred thousand," and added quickly, "but I'll take it."

The contracts were initialed and signed. We all shook hands and congratulated each other. Mr. and Mrs. O'Brien were happy with the price, and Martha and I were happy we would get our commissions. Loretta must be happy since she did not have to meet Richard's price. I asked to use the phone again. I told Loretta the final outcome and said I would be right over to get their initials on the new changes to the contract. As I was driving I thought, Loretta must be pleased she didn't have to pay the two hundred thousand dollars Richard wanted. I hope Louis is happy too. They were all glad to see me. We finished the paperwork and I said, "I will get the contracts to your attorney. Who are you using?"

"Louis's cousin is an attorney. His office is in Newark." Loretta paused and smiled at Louis. "Louis will get the contract to Antonio. I'll give you his name and phone number."

"Okay great. Now how about the mortgage?"

"I'll be in touch with Ralph tomorrow morning and then I'll call you."

"Here is the information on the O'Brien's attorney. The two lawyers can go over anything they feel is necessary to be clarified." I was anxious to get home. It had been a long, long day.

The following day at about half past four I realized I had not heard from Loretta. The financial service representative stopped by my office to see how the offer had gone. "It went great, the owners settled for $197,000. We just need the attorney's approval and the mortgage commitment."

"Congratulations."

"Save that until the closing. Anything can happen between now and then."

"Let me know how the mortgage turns out. He really is very low on everything."

I called Loretta's office but she was not in. I left a message on her home phone. It was a little after five and I left the office. I thought, "If she doesn't call me tonight I'll catch her at the office tomorrow, before the weekend begins."

I stopped at my brother's and had dinner with him and his wife. We talked about the stock market being down and the slow housing market. I told them I had a signed contract. When I mentioned the price they were shocked it was so high. After a glass of wine I left for home. As I walked in the door, the phone was ringing, but it was not Loretta. I made an appointment with the caller to show them a house the next day. It was nine o'clock, time to put on my robe and relax. I checked the phone messages but there was nothing from Loretta.

The next day was Friday. Friday is a strange day in the real estate world. As far as the mortgage brokers, bankers, and attorneys go, it is a dead day. Whatever you communicate or forward to them will get no action until Monday. So I knew if Loretta didn't have any information about the mortgage I would have to wait until Monday to try to speed things up.

At nine o'clock, just before leaving for the office, I called her at work.

"This is Loretta."

"Good morning, I'm so glad I'm able to reach you." I could tell from the deep breath I heard her take she was surprised to hear my voice. "I've been anxious to hear how the mortgage is progressing."

I waited a minute before saying anything more. Loretta hesitated, "I've been trying to get in touch with the mortgage broker." I didn't say anything. I waited. "Ah—he hasn't gotten back to me."

The Cat and Mouse Game

This did not sound like the confident, arrogant, and pushy Loretta I had encountered a few days ago. I sensed that something was wrong.

"It's Friday. If you can't get to him on Monday, let me know. You only have ten days to make a good faith effort to get a mortgage. Did Louis get the contract to your attorney?"

"Yes, we did that the next evening."

"Did he go over everything with you? Did he have any questions?"

"No, he found everything in order."

"The contract also has a deadline for your attorney to get in touch with the seller's attorney." I suggested it was advisable that they have a friendly relationship. "If you have no luck reaching the mortgage broker on Monday, you might ask your attorney to call him."

Once the contracts are signed, time limits are set. If they are not adhered to, the contract may be broken and the buyer can lose the right to purchase the property. Occasionally buyers do not realize this. Sometimes they waste time running from one bank to another or contacting various mortgage brokers. Time slips by and the options are gone. This is why having the financial service representative available at the signing of the contract is so helpful. As soon as it is accepted the representative can start processing the loan.

My weekend was very busy. I had a couple from New York City who were anxious to leave the confusion of Manhattan and the brick walls their apartment looked out on to. The husband and wife were both attorneys and were able to afford a home in the range of three hundred thousand dollars. We looked at four wonderful houses but nothing moved them enough to make an offer. They were so unlike the Rodriquez's who showed their approval openly. The lawyers were extremely hard to read. I didn't think this was going to be a quick sale. On Sunday, I had early morning floor time. One call developed into an appointment. My day ended at about half past four.

Monday morning I decided I had to get involved with Loretta's mortgage broker. At ten o'clock I called her.

"Good morning Loretta, have you had a chance to call about the mortgage?"

"He's not at his office. I left word for him to call me."

"Loretta I think he is avoiding you. It has been three days that you have been leaving messages for him. Something is wrong."

Very defensively, "What do you mean? What could be wrong?"

"Have you filled out an application with him or was everything done on the phone?"

"We talked on the phone."

"Would you mind if I called to find out what is going on?"

"If he's not there I don't understand what you can do." Begrudgingly she gave me his name and phone number.

When his office answered, the receptionist asked who was calling. I gave her my name and Ralph answered the phone. I told him I was with Opportunity Realtors, but it did not ring a bell for him. I asked him what his best rate was for a thirty-year mortgage with a 30 percent down payment. The rate was a full point higher than he had quoted to Loretta.

"Do you remember speaking with Mrs. Rodriquez?"

There was a noticeable pause. "Yes, I do."

"That's not what you quoted to her."

"No, I made a mistake." He was new at this business and sounded embarrassed.

"She has been trying to reach you for three days. I know you just started in this business and you will make mistakes. The best way to handle a mistake is to face it head on."

He responded with a very shy, "Yes."

"Because you have not returned her calls we have wasted three valuable days." I continued to speak with him and learned that this would have been his first mortgage placement.

The Cat and Mouse Game

He said, "She was so determined to get a low rate and low points. I guess I got carried away. Believe me, this will never happen again. I just hate to call her back and tell her I can't do it."

"I'll leave that up to you, but I have to call her. We must decide where to go for a mortgage." He told me he was sorry for the way it turned out.

I called Loretta and tried to explain that he could not follow through. She was very upset. "Now, what are we going to do?"

"We had ten days to show that we were having a mortgage processed. Three days are gone. Do you have anyone else in mind for the loan?"

"No, I don't. I'll have to talk to my father this evening. We have wasted enough time on this."

I didn't think I had wasted time getting to the bottom of the problem. There was no "Thank you for following through for me." Now I knew what I had to do. I walked to the financial service representative's office and told Ms. Silver that Loretta might be back to her. The low mortgage rate and points quoted were no longer available. "If you want to give it a try, why not do some work on the figures before she contacts you. See what the best rate and points will be."

"I have all the information that Loretta and Louis gave me. I'll start on it right now."

"When you get it all put together, I'll tell you what happened with Loretta's mortgage broker."

"I'd love to hear," she chuckled.

I had letters to get out and a few phone calls to make. Later I had lunch with some of my sales associates. We all had some kind of problem to talk about. Real estate takes many hours of planning even before starting to show property to a client. You must have knowledge about the school system, the tax structure, rail and bus transportation, and the availability of money—all this before zeroing in on the area. The type of house, number of bedrooms, and the size of property can all be a challenge. It's good to exchange ideas with your coworkers. Mary needed an inexpensive colonial with three bedrooms, but couldn't find one. "I will be listing something that might fill the bill for you," I told her.

"LuLu, as soon as you get it let me know. My clients are very anxious."

The rest of the day disappeared. I was at home and had just finished dinner when the phone rang. I was sure it would be Loretta. "Hello?"

"LuLu, do you know what mortgage rates your financial service representative has?" I wanted to say, "Aha you're back to my financial service representative are you," but I didn't.

"The rates and points change every day, Loretta. Have you and your father checked around today?"

"Sort of."

Only six days were left to finalize a mortgager. We had to do something quickly. "Let's meet at my office in about an hour and see what Ms. Silver has to offer you and Louis." I thought I better start including him in the transaction.

"An hour and a half will be a little better for us. I'll see you then."

I called Ms. Silver to see if she would be available. She would be there in an hour. We both arrived at the same time and went to her office. She had all the figures worked out. The rate was the same as when Loretta was first there, but she was able to reduce the points. Since she didn't have to meet or beat the phony rate, the drop in points may be just enough to sway Loretta and her father to Ms. Silver. She felt good about what she had to offer.

As Loretta, Louis, and the father walked in I said, "I'm so happy you came in this evening and that Ms. Silver is able to be here. If we had to wait until the end of your business day tomorrow we would have used up half of the time needed to process the mortgage. So let's get started."

"Yes, I'm tired of all this. I want to get it over with!" Loretta was still very abrupt and defiant. We walked to the financial service representative's office. I knew they were in good hands.

A few minutes later Martha came in. "I saw your buyers coming out of the National Bank about a half an hour ago. Are they placing the mortgage there?"

"No. I think they were shopping. They're in with Silver now."

When they were leaving her office I heard Loretta say, "Your rate is the same as everyone else but the points are better. Do you have enough time to get this done for the closing?" From her tone it sounded as though she doubted Silver's ability; not the fact that it was her fault that time was running out.

Finally that was out of the way! "Please come back to my office. I want to ask you a few questions." She looked exhausted. Her father was not as talkative as before. Louis was smiling. "How is your attorney doing? Has he spoken to the O'Brien's attorney?"

She looked at Louis and he said, "This is my cousin's first real estate closing in the United States. He was a lawyer in Puerto Rico."

"Oh, I see."

Yes, there was another problem. The new lawyer needed a great deal of help. No, they did not close on time. But after much aggravation, short tempers, and anxiety it did close and I received my commission.

What a wonderful transaction this would have been if Loretta had worked with Ms. Silver and one of our recommended real estate attorneys from the start. I really cannot complain because they bought the one and only house I showed them. But with much aggravation!

CHAPTER 8

It's All In the Family

And then there was the time I was renting an apartment, which was being converted into condominium ownership. I bought two units and suggested to my brother, "Why don't you buy one? They will only go up in value. We are in on the ground floor." Joe did buy one and for a while was a landlord. He sold his unit after a few years and was happy with the return on his investment.

My niece Jeanne also bought one of the units. After she finished decorating, it had a lot of charm. When she was ready to move the selling price brought her a good return. I then sold her a darling colonial where she stayed for a short while. Again she painted and decorated in an appealing way and I was able to find a buyer for her. She was pleased with the equity realized on this sale also.

A second niece Susan and her husband purchased a wonderful ten-room colonial with a huge swimming pool. The interior decorator arrived and transformed a tired house into a wonderful home.

A third niece Kathy and her husband heard of a condominium in a great area that was for sale. There was a very unpleasant divorce going on between the owners and it was under foreclosure. The unit had broken windows, broken locks on the doors, it was dirty, and there were overdue utility and mortgage payments. I was able to work out all the problems in this very ugly situation and the closing occurred after some delay. Gradually two new bathrooms were installed, the decorating was completed, and wall-to-wall carpeting helped to make a world of difference. Three children later, my niece and her husband are still living there.

I sold my nephew, Joseph, a small condo. This was after a few years of thinking about purchasing. He was a cautious buyer but is very satisfied with his purchase.

So you see, family can be extremely important and helpful.

CHAPTER 9

A Gift of a Deal

Real estate is such a strange, frustrating, exasperating, and wonderful business. Wonderful when all the pieces fall together perfectly, like a jigsaw puzzle, when you finish and there are no pieces left. A "gift of a deal" is when you show a buyer one house and they buy that house—that's super wonderful. In twenty-five years of selling there have not been too many times when I have had a "gift of a deal." One year I had two "gifts."

It was Saturday and I had just walked into my real estate office when I was paged. The receptionist said there was a phone call for me. I answered, "This is LuLu, how may I help you?"

A young woman said, "We saw your name on a sign on Sycamore Avenue and would like to see that house." What a break that I had just arrived. If I hadn't been in, someone else would have met with this buyer.

"When would you like to see it?" I was ready to go that minute, but I tried to sound calm.

"We are at the Town Pub having a burger. How about in an hour?" Her voice was very sweet with a slight, interesting accent.

"That sounds great. I'll meet you at the house in one hour."

The property they called on was a pretty English-type colonial that had been well kept through the years. The lot was small, but so were all the others in the area. The living and dining rooms were large, with lovely oak trim. The

A Gift of a Deal

kitchen was older but also a decent size. There was no powder room on the first floor and the main bath was old. The three bedrooms were the usual sizes, one large, one medium, and a small one. The basement and attic were unfinished. It was a nice house, good for a young couple to start out in. They would probably want to do some updating.

It was a lovely spring day, perfect for looking at houses. I arrived at the house a little ahead of time so I could make sure everything was in order. I unlocked the door, turned on some lights, and was ready to greet the young couple. They were on time, which was nice. Not all buyers are on time.

"My name is LuLu, I'll be happy to show you the property."

He said, "Great, we were in the neighborhood when we saw the sign. My name is Juan and this is my wife Maria."

It wasn't long before I knew that they were from Union City, a small town filled with immigrants and crowded streets. It was across the river from New York City. They had been married for five years. She liked the size of the rooms and loved the furnishings. They both agreed the wallpaper on the first floor was attractive. That meant they would not have to redecorate those rooms. On the second floor the first door was to the old bathroom. I thought they would find fault but he only said, "We would have to do a little work in here." She agreed and walked on to the bedrooms. Next to the master bedroom was an unheated, enclosed porch.

I suggested, "With some electric heat out here, this will make a nice office or a second floor TV room."

"Juan, you could use this for your office when you bring work home from the bank."

They liked the size of the other bedrooms. The attic was very large and for some reason it held a particular appeal for him. Maybe he was thinking of an office up there. In the basement, really an old cellar, we talked about the laundry area and if the washer and dryer were included. He asked about the heating unit, the age and what the heating bills were. "I will be happy to find out the age for you. The person who lived here was older and probably had it warmer than you would like."

"I would appreciate that and you are probably right about the temperature."

At this point I left them alone to talk. I went upstairs to be out of the way. They seemed to like the house, but I have had this reaction so many times. If it doesn't materialize into a sale it really doesn't matter how much they like it. When Maria and Juan came upstairs I asked, "Do you have any questions? What do you think of the house?"

Two very excited people said in unison, "We like it very much."

He said, "We would like our parents to see it. Do you think you could show it to them tomorrow about four o'clock?"

Oh boy, here comes "the kiss of death." That's what I call it when the parents come to "help." I've seen it so many times. The parents remember what they paid for their home, probably twenty years ago. Mentally, they compare all they have to what has to be done, to the overpriced house that the realtor is trying to force on their children. This is the usual protective attitude of some parents.

I took a deep breath and with an assuring smile said, "I'd be happy to meet them here at four o'clock tomorrow." Since they lived in another county I asked, "Do you know how to get back home?"

"Oh we have friends who just bought a house on the next block, so we know our way, thank you."

This was a plus for me! When buyers know someone in the area, many times it will draw them to that location. Maybe their parents wouldn't find too many faults.

When some "helpful" parents come into a house, the minute I see their faces, I know if it's a bummer. They look glum, no smiles, and they check out every hairline crack in the ceilings. I often wonder how many of their ceilings are in perfect condition. I used to try to explain or minimize each problem the parents came up with. But that doesn't stop them. They find something else. If the parents are helping with the down payment it's a no-win situation for me. My method of handling this now is to walk into the next room and let the young couple point out what they like about the house. Any real problems will be settled by negotiating and through the attorneys. My motto is "live in hope" and maybe their parents will like it too.

Maria and Juan were great to work with. The next day they were all at the house waiting for me when I arrived. I was on time, but I had the feeling they were anxious to show off the inside of the house to their parents. The introductions were made and we went in. "Why don't you take your parents through the house and point out all the nice things that you like about it." I made myself busy by turning on the lights.

Their families were delightful. They were all smiles as they walked through the house. This was a good sign. I could hear bits of conversation, "I like the wallpaper and the dining room is so big. We'll change the kitchen cabinets." So far everything seemed to be going very well.

"Can we go down to the basement?" I told them the lights were on and that they could go down. Now the interesting questions start. "Do they get water in the cellar? Are there termites? How old is the heating unit?" At this time I point out that most buyers have engineering, radon, and termite inspections done. In this way, all their questions will be answered professionally. We talked a little more and then they went outside to see the garage and the property. I asked if they were finished looking inside. When they said they were, I excused myself to lock up the house.

At the front of the property Juan said, "I would like to talk with my family. I'll call you in the morning."

We all said our good-byes. I knew that the young couple was very excited about the house. The parents seemed to be the type who would be happy with whatever their children wanted. It was nice to see parents who were not negative and fault finding. But one never knows. Now they will talk about price, what they feel has to be done to the property, and if they get real fussy, they will find fault with the old kitchen and the old bathroom, in which the ceiling paint is peeling. The fact that there is no powder room on the first floor will be discussed. This is a very big drawback in the sale of a house.

A Gift of a Deal

On the plus side, it is a very nice family street and a short walk to a wonderful park, which has jogging trails and tennis courts. Transportation to New York City is just two blocks away.

Back at the office on Monday, a call came in from Juan. They wanted to see me about seven o'clock to go over some details. As before they were prompt and we went to a conference room. He informed me that several months ago they had made an offer on a house in another area, so they were rather familiar with the process of putting together a contract. The price is where the challenge comes into play. They also knew from their prior experience that our office represents the seller.

"What price do you think you would like to offer the owner?"

They looked at each other and Juan started, "You know, we like the house very much." I nodded my head. "But there are a few things we will have to do to it and that will take money."

"No house is perfect," I smiled at them trying to put them at ease. "Just make an offer you feel comfortable with, keeping in mind that the owner has to be happy too."

There is a story within this story. The owner of this house is the mother of a very close friend. She had lived in the house for fifty years and now is in a nursing home. Her daughter, Monica, has power of attorney. When it was first decided that the house must be sold, Monica mentioned her intentions to me. I suggested that she put an advertisement in the newspaper and a sign on the property, which she did. I indicated a price but she decided on her own price, which was higher. This is a normal reaction. Most sellers think their home is worth more than a professional's opinion.

She had a few calls inquiring about the property. One person wanted to rent it. The daughter of a neighbor loved it, but could not afford the price. A realtor called to list it.

Then it was in limbo for several weeks. I suggested she list the property with me. Monica felt, maybe hoped, something would develop with the calls she had received. I offered to follow through on the two prospects, since she had not done this, to see if there was any serious interest. Following through, that is calling back the people who have answered the ads, is difficult to do unless you are trained in the procedure. I learned that the neighbor's daughter truly could not afford the house. From the realtor friend who called for the listing, I learned the second person calls on many advertisements but never follows through. When working with a stranger to obtain a listing this is not the procedure I practice. I was trying to use my experience to help Monica sell her mother's house as quickly as possible for the best price. No one needs an extra house to heat and maintain through the winter. After much discussion and using the sale prices of properties in the area as a comparative analysis, I finally listed the house for $178,000. A "For Sale" sign went up immediately with my name on it.

The following day Maria called to see the house. I was about to get an offer on a house that had been listed for only two days! I could hear a voice in my mind saying, "Monica is going to tell you it should have been listed higher." The comparative market analysis that I worked up showed the price in keeping with area sales.

All these thoughts flashed through my mind as I looked at Juan while he nervously said, "We would like to offer $165,000." There was a slight pause as he went on, "But if she does not take it we would like the opportunity to make another offer." He explained his reasoning, "With the other house that we lost out on we did not have a chance to go up in our price."

They were such a nice, sincere couple I couldn't help liking them. He was the assistant treasurer at a bank in New York City. She worked for a fashion designer in the city. I

A Gift of a Deal 77

would love for them to be able to buy the house, but the price—I had to think of my seller's needs. I knew the money would be used for the nursing home expenses.

"I will present the offer this evening. I am sure that there will be a counteroffer, at which time you will have an opportunity to make a second offer." He seemed to relax when I told him this. "I'll tell them that you are well qualified to obtain a mortgage and that you have been at your jobs for five or more years. All of these facts are in your favor." I asked them to sign the offer and to give me a check for the earnest money. "I will call now to make an appointment for this evening. As soon as I have an answer I'll get back to you."

I had already explained to them about having inspections done for the structure, radon, and termite conditions. They had names of people who had been suggested to them. I guessed they were from their friends who had just bought on the next block. So far everything was going along beautifully. I had a buyer who qualified and was anxious to buy this house.

Now for the hardest part. The seller always wants more money and the buyer always wants to give less. Here is where this realtor earns her commission trying to make two couples happy. If you think this is easy, you're wrong. When it is family or a friend it takes a lot of patience and a lot of selling psychology in order to pull it all together. I arrived at Monica's home, coming in through the back door, much different than going to the front door of an unknown owner and a little less formal, but just as serious and professional.

As I walked in I said, "I told you I thought they were interested." Monica and her husband were smiling, anticipating a good offer I'm sure. "They are so lovely, not only do they like the house they like your mother's furnishings." I paused and could see that she was pleased to hear that. "They asked me to find out if you will be having a house sale."

Her answer was quick, "There wouldn't be anything left when all the grandchildren and my sister put in their requests."

"In any event, they have made an offer. They have given me a deposit check of one thousand dollars." I paused so they would realize the buyers were sincere. "I want you to know that they are very well qualified for a mortgage. They have been working at their jobs for over five years." I wished she could have met Juan and Maria before I had an offer, because I know she would have approved of this couple. We were sitting around a table in the TV room. "Take a look at the contracts." As with all sellers their eyes quickly scanned the typing looking for the dollar amount. "They are offering $165,000."

Monica shook her head and said, "No, that's not what I want." She started to hand back the contract.

I didn't reach out for it and said, "I didn't think you would accept it, but I am legally obligated to present it to you." I paused again to impress upon her that this is a legal obligation. Very slowly I said, "Now, you have the opportunity to give them a counteroffer. Don't turn your back on an interested buyer."

The two of them had a short conversation and she said, "I really want the full price." I reminded her that the house across the street sold for $170,000 and that it had a new kitchen and a new bath.

"What about that other young couple I mentioned to you who were interested?" Monica asked.

They were an exception to the contract. Sometimes, when the owner has tried to sell on their own and think one of the "lookers" might be interested, a realtor will make them an exception to the sale. There would be no commission to the realtor. Monica was still hoping she could sell the house herself.

"I think I told you I spoke to her and they could not afford it." Had Monica been a stranger I would have suggested, "Counter with $172,000," but I didn't want to appear too "pushy." That's a word I hear when trying to be helpful. "Do you want to think about it and give me an answer tomorrow?" This would take some of the tension out of the situation. She could talk to her family.

They looked at each other. Her husband was being very smart. It was her mother's house and he knew it should be her decision. "Okay," she said, "we'll talk to you tomorrow." It's like walking on thin ice when you deal with a good friend or a relative. You want to help but you can't be too forceful. They have to feel it is their decision. So I decided to back off.

I arrived home a little before ten o'clock and called Maria and Juan immediately. I knew they would be waiting to hear from me. "Hi, Juan, I hope it's not too late to call."

"No way, we were hoping to hear from you before we went to bed. We're not going to be able to sleep anyway. What did she have to say?" Before I could answer, Juan said, "Wait 'till Maria gets on the other phone."

In a minute she said, "Okay I'm here."

I told them I had informed Monica about their ability to qualify for a mortgage. Then I told them what they really wanted to hear. "She's looking for a little more money, but wants to think about it overnight. When she gives me her counteroffer you can decide what you want to do." I waited for a response but all I heard was a deep sigh. "The occupancy was fine. It will give her time to get everything out of the house."

I didn't say she wanted full price because she was going to think about it. With some contracts the closing date can be a stumbling block. Sometimes a good potential sale can fall apart because of timing. Here, I had a seller deciding how much more she would like to get and buyers wondering how much higher they would have to go. I'm sure the buyers and the seller had a restless night. I didn't have any trouble sleeping because I knew the buyers would increase their offer.

Early the next morning I had a call. Monica had decided that $172,000 was the counteroffer. I called Juan at his office and told him the news. Without a moments hesitation he said, "We will offer $170,000." I knew they must have made up their minds about the price last night. His answer was so quick and firm. "Please tell her that there is a lot of work that has to be done. I'm not trying to insult her. For a young person's needs the kitchen and bathroom have to be remodeled. We can use the extra two thousand dollars for modernizing."

I couldn't help noticing how sensitive he was when he said, "I am not trying to insult her." I have dealt with people who are very nasty when they are trying to ram an offer down an owner's throat. This was really a lovely young couple. I knew he was right because Monica and I had already talked over these points.

I asked when he and Maria could come to the office to initial the changes. Then, if their offer was accepted, the contract would be complete. "This evening at seven will be good."

True to his word they were there, again on time. The changes were made and initialed. I explained that if the offer was accepted the seller's attorney would review the contract and make any changes he felt necessary. Then he would contact the buyer's attorney. They would work out the differences. When this was completed the inspections would be ordered. If there were no problems, he and his wife would then apply for their mortgage. I had touched on all the details with them. I felt comfortable and they had no questions.

We parted and I contacted Monica. I had to go over the new offer with Monica and her husband and reconfirm the closing date. At this point the question always comes up, "What amount will be left after all the deductions?" We were in the TV room talking about the rain that had just started. "Let's sit at the table, so I can go over all the figures with you." I told Monica that I would speak to her mother's attorney. We went over the fact that the buyer would have engineering, termite, and radon inspections done.

"I'm not paying for any of those inspections to be done." I assured her she was not.

"But, if a problem is found we will have to talk about how it would be rectified." I handed them each a copy of the contract. "They are coming back with an offer of $170,000. Juan feels there is work to be done in the kitchen and bathroom, and they will need a powder room on the first floor." I saw she was hesitating. "I think they are going to stay with this figure."

She started again to tell me she thought it was worth more. "It's a nice area, close to New York transportation and schools." I understood how she felt. It had been the house she grew up in. She was not quite ready to give it up.

I had to put a little pressure on now. "Monica, if the house is so wonderful and priced so well, why haven't you had any other offers in the last six weeks since you put your sign up and ran the ads in the paper?" I was trying to be realistic. Sometimes our sentiments interfere with our thinking.

"Well, what do you think I should do?"

"I think you should take the offer. You have good buyers, with a good down payment. They have nothing to sell to hold up the closing."

She still hesitated. "I'll call my attorney in the morning." I told her I thought that was a good idea. I knew he would advise her to take the offer.

I was happy to get home. It had been a long day. The tension was beginning to build up in my neck and back.

The following day in mid afternoon Monica called. "If you would like to pick up the contract it is signed. I spoke to my lawyer and he said he would talk with you."

"That's great Monica. By Christmas, all this will be behind you."

I left the office as fast as I could, picked up the contract, and was back in my office faxing it to the seller's attorney, expecting to do the same with the buyer's attorney. I called to get their fax number but no one answered the phone. I called repeatedly and finally someone answered. "We have no fax. I can make arrangements for you to send it to a nearby office."

I began to wonder what kind of a "Mickey Mouse" law office we were dealing with. At the contract signing I had suggested several local real estate lawyers. But Juan's father-in-law had recommended this attorney. I was not about to say the wrong thing at this point. The seller's attorney was someone Monica's father had used. They had business dealings for many years, long before her father had died. A young associate with the firm was handling the sale for the senior partner. He knew what he was doing, but the buyer's lawyer was never available and did not follow up. They finally did agree to a few minor changes.

The inspections would now start. The termite inspection did reveal termite damage. It had to be treated and some carpentry work was also needed. The engineer's report was favorable but the radon reading revealed a very high number. Oh well, I thought, this was it! I knew it was too good to be true. I showed them only one house and they loved it. Now it looked shaky. Some people get nervous and will walk away from this kind of a radon reading. It can be remedied with a fan system, but at a cost of several hundred dollars. Monica had told me that since she came down on the price she hoped there would not be any other expenses that would be her liability. The termite treatment is the seller's responsibility, so there was no way out of that.

"Why do I have to pay for the treatment?" Monica asked. "If they want it done, let them pay for it."

"Monica, the bank will not approve the mortgage without a certificate stating that the work has been done."

"What about the radon? My mother lived in the house for fifty years and is now ninety years old. It didn't bother her."

A Gift of a Deal

"I know that. I have told Juan and Maria this. In order to sell the house, you have to do it. If you refuse and they walk away from the sale, the house goes back on the market. If you are lucky enough to get another buyer before the winter sets in, the new buyer will also have the radon test done. You will be back to the same situation."

"How much is it going to cost?"

"I don't know. In twenty-three years I have never sold a house where the reading has been this high. Something has to be done." I felt sorry for her. Here was another expense eating into the money needed for her mother's care. "I called the Building Department hoping someone would have some knowledge of radon reports in the area. I asked about the neighbors across the street, who just sold their house. I learned their reading was average. So there is no accounting for where radon will manifest itself."

"So, what do I do next?"

Part of a realtor's responsibility is to help and direct. "I think maybe it's a good idea for you to have another reading done. There is always the possibility of an error. If your reading is the same as the buyer's, you have no choice."

She liked my idea. Another test was done. It takes five to seven days before the results are mailed back. In the meantime Juan was calling almost everyday to find out if the work was going to be done. When the results came back there was a significant difference in the reading. With this result, the buyer opted to have a third reading done. A third week went by while we waited for the results. This is an example of why closings are delayed. Until situations like this are decided, the buyer usually does not apply for a mortgage. The result of the third reading was slightly lower than the first but not low enough. The work had to be done to rectify the situation. I was later told that readings do fluctuate as the gas is released. Even the weather can influence a reading.

"What do I do now? Who does this kind of work?" Monica asked.

I suggested a company to Monica who had done an inspection and correction for me a few weeks earlier. "You can also look in the yellow pages. This way you can get a few estimates." It is very difficult to refer subcontractors. I always try to suggest several reputable lawyers, engineers, and pest control people so the decision is theirs, not mine.

I was busy with a few other transactions so I left the appointment making to Monica. Needless to say, time had to be spent on the phone. Small contractors are usually out on jobs during the day, so several calls must be made before you reach them. If they are busy, you do not always get a call back. They just ignore you. While all of this was going on, the buyer called me everyday. He wanted to know if the work had started.

A week later I received a call from Monica. "This is enough, I can't wait around for these men to call me back."

I was a little surprised, "No one has returned your calls?"

"Your man, what's his name, called and met me. He gave me a price but no one else has called me back. If you think he is good, I'll go with him."

"He is certified by the state. He's been in this business quite a few years. So I would assume he knows what is required."

It was decided that she could not waste any more time on this project. She had to visit her mother at the nursing home, food shop, walk the dog, and play a little golf. So the day went by quickly without having to spend time calling contractors. I advised her to call her attorney to inform him that she had decided to go ahead with the required work. He would call the buyer's attorney and then the buyer's attorney would go ahead with the mortgage application for his client. Because of the delay, due to the additional radon inspections, the closing was changed from October fifteenth to the twenty-ninth of October.

I was beginning to relax a little since all the inspections had been done. The termite, carpenter, and radon people were doing their work. Only one item had to be completed. It was the most important one, the mortgage. But I had nothing to be concerned about. The buyer's attorney, the attorney of their choice, was handling that.

Juan called almost every day to check on the progress at the house. I asked him how the mortgage was going and he assured me it was under control. As we drew closer to the October twenty-ninth closing date, I attempted to reach the buyer's attorney to zero in on the exact time of the closing. As in the past, I had a difficult time getting someone on the phone. About five days prior to the closing, I finally reached an assistant, only to find out that a mortgage commitment had not been received.

Juan and Maria had given their landlord notice that they would be out of the apartment by the first of November. Now, because of the delay with the mortgage, they would have to move out of their apartment, put things in storage, and live temporarily with her family. There are situations when a closing must be delayed. This attorney wanted to control the mortgage. The application process should have started once the sellers agreed to do all the necessary work. The buyers would have to move twice in a matter of weeks. I kept in touch with Juan to make sure he was making some progress with the mortgage. Normally I stay in contact with the bank or mortgage company to keep things moving along and to know at what point the process is. But with this attorney, it was impossible to make contact. I kept prodding Juan. Originally the attorney promised Juan the rate would be half of 1 percent less than I could find for him. That was the reason he went along with the attorney his father-in-law had suggested and not the mortgage specialist I had recommended. Now that so much time had passed since the original quote, the rate was higher. It was about this time, when we didn't know the closing date or the mortgage rate, that Juan said, "Maybe I should have used the lawyer you suggested."

I felt sad that they were being inconvenienced at a time that should be a happy experience. I wanted to say, "Yes, you should have. I've had lots of experience with lawyers." I didn't tell him that. Instead I said, "Before you know it, you will be in your new home. Just keep after your attorney. Call him every other day. Let me know when you hear the closing date." Ten more days went by and we were in the first week of November. The lawyers settled on November twelfth, almost a month late, for the closing.

Since the closing was in another county, I picked Monica up and drove to her lawyer's office. We had an enjoyable ride going over some of the problems that had occurred but admitted that the goal to sell before winter came was achieved. We arrived on time at the lawyer's office and spent some time in idle talk with the senior attorney who then introduced us to the young partner who would handle the closing. We went into the reception room and waited.

If you haven't guessed it, the buyers and their lawyer were late, a half hour late. They had never been to the area and were lost. There were apologies and introductions. We all went into a large conference room and sat around a ten-foot-long table. Mr. St. Claire, Monica's attorney, sat at one end. We sat next to him on the long side of the table. Next to us sat Juan and Maria. The entire other side of the table, all ten feet, was used by the buyer's attorney, Mr. Lopez, for his papers. The assistant arranged them in layers of three or four sheets in about eight or ten sections, a most unusual arrangement. The assistant did not sit down. He moved back and forth delivering each set of papers to Mr. Lopez. I have never before seen a performance like this. I hope I never do again. When all the papers were signed I congratulated the new owners and presented them with a gift for their new home.

Monica wished them happiness and hoped they would enjoy their new home. As soon as the checks were handed out, Monica and I left.

When I show one house to a buyer and they sign a contract I say it is truly a gift. But no gift comes without strings attached to it. Now all the strings were tied up into a big bow.

A few months later I had a call from Juan. "I think we need a local attorney. What is the name of the attorney you wanted to recommend to us?" I was happy to provide him with three local, experienced lawyers.

One Sunday, a short time later, I met the happy homeowners at church. They were anxious to tell me their good news. "We are going to have a baby!"

"How wonderful! We have a saying in real estate, 'a new home, a new baby.'" I was very pleased for them. It will be the first baby in thirty-two years in the cute English Tudor. No longer will the house be quiet while the original owner dreams of past years. The house will be alive again with young voices and dreams of the future.

CHAPTER 10

The Three-year Contract

When I was selling real estate in New Jersey, a young woman named Katie called my office asking to see newly constructed homes. My selling area of Essex County was in an older, built-up location. There were a few leftover lots that had been subdivided from larger properties. Newly built homes were not a common sight.

"I want to be close to Route 3 because it is near the town in which our business is located. The commute would be good for my husband and me."

I explained that if she would consider going a little farther west I would have a number of properties to show her. Because of the closeness to New York City, this area had been a prime location for the "big city" employees and it was densely populated.

"No, I don't want to spend any more than a half hour in traveling time."

Well, that took care of what could have been a potential buyer. "I do have a cul-de-sac on which two new homes have been built. I'll be happy to show them to you."

"I'd rather have the address. Then if I like the area I will make an appointment with you."

I knew there was always a chance that this type of buyer might be tempted to go directly to the builder, in which case I would not earn a commission. I was willing to take the chance because the builder was now working in another town and might not be easy to reach. She sounded very impatient. So I decided to take my chances.

The Three-year Contract

"I'll be happy to tell you where the houses are located. They are about eight minutes from Route 3." I asked for her name, address, and phone number. "I will mail you information on these houses and on a few of the new houses in the next community." I took care of the mailing and tried to concentrate on my appointments for the day. I wished that the call could have worked into an appointment, but that didn't look possible.

The following week I called Katie to see if she had any interest in the houses on the cul-de-sac. "Oh, *no* I wouldn't be interested in any thing like *that*. I want a new area with new houses all around me."

There was no doubt by the tone of her voice that she was not interested. Katie was a cash buyer in the two- to three-hundred-thousand-dollar price range. Mentally I was calculating what my commission could be. The problem was that there was no acreage in the area for a subdivision of new houses. Well, it was a good try.

"Katie, I think I know what you want. I will keep you in mind and let you know as soon as anything comes along that meets your requirements." She was very professional and definite in her requirements. We had a pleasant talk, but in the back of my mind I was thinking, there's no way for this to happen. She either has to move farther out or change her mind about a *new* house if she wants a convenient commute.

Several months went by and much to my surprise there was a realtor "open house" for four newly built houses. I rushed out to see them. They turned out to be the start of a new subdivision that I was not aware of. The perfect location for that caller who wanted to be near Route 3! I thought the houses were wonderful, with beautiful kitchens and new styles in the bathrooms. They had a unique design new to this area. There was an open, airy flair to the architecture that one sees in the finer homes in Florida. The many floor to ceiling windows were very different from the older colonial homes nearby. Portions of three towns made up this last, buildable acreage in the area. The property was hidden with overgrowth, sitting high on a ridge over the road. It was in a quarry area and it would be necessary to blast to construct the foundations. Perhaps that's why, through the years, houses had not been built there. It was across the street from a bird sanctuary. I had always thought this was part of that preserve.

I knew Katie would love the homes and the location, if she had not already bought something. Now to find the telephone number she had given to me. At the time we first spoke a sale sounded so impossible. I wondered if I kept the file with her information. Fortunately I have learned to save records, names, telephone numbers, and bits of information about buyers. It's important to know what they want or need. I was lucky! I had saved the information. When I called Katie and started to describe the location and the houses, she sounded just as excited as I was.

We made plans to meet that evening after dinner. Katie and her husband, Greg, had no problem finding the site. The builder's agent was there and we introduced ourselves. We started to inspect the four models. Each one had some unique quality, but one by one they were rejected, until we came to the last house. I could immediately tell that they both loved it. We talked about the openness of the design, the arched windows, the traffic flow, and the color of the marble in the kitchen. The kitchen was almost breathtaking. When you have sold old houses for fifteen years and have seen cabinets and countertops that you would love to pull out and redo, this construction was exciting.

"I'm not too keen on the black-gray effect of the marble. I really like the green marble in the ranch house we were just in."

The builder's agent, Terry, came to the rescue, "That's not a problem. If you wish, we can change the kitchen and bathroom cabinets, the tub and sink colors, and the lighting fixtures."

The Three-year Contract 91

"I really don't like the quality of the cabinets," Katie told her.

"As I said, we can change, upgrade, or eliminate. It's up to you" was the agent's response.

At this point I intervened, "Terry why don't we go to your office where you have some samples? Katie and Greg will need to look at the plot plan to see the location of the available lots. That way they can decide what property will be good for them."

We continued to talk about more changes as we walked to her office. There were samples of kitchen and bathroom tiles, a choice of wood trim designs, and various woods for flooring. Katie saw the perfect tile! Of course it was an upgrade. She thought the spindles on the stairs were too far apart. She was worried that her little boy, Teddy, would be able to get his head between them. That was no problem; add one spindle on each step, "at an added cost." As the conversation went on, I reached the distinct impression that money was no problem.

Their little boy became restless and our thoughts were interrupted over and over. I said, "Katie, I know it's difficult for you to make decisions now. When can you come in to talk about the details without Teddy?"

"That can be arranged. He goes to nursery school. I'll leave the office early and I can meet you here. My husband will go along with almost anything I decide."

"That's true, she has very good taste," Greg agreed. "Katie decorated our town house and it's beautiful."

Looking at me, the listing agent said, "I will be happy to do all of the work with Katie for the extras and upgrades. We can go to the carpet showroom. She can decide on cabinets, fixtures, and colors. When we have a contract, I will send you a copy." Since Terry's office was at the building site, she worked very closely with the builder.

Katie looked at me and said, "Do you mind?"

Did I mind? I loved it! "As long as you are happy and get the things you want Katie, that's all that matters. If anything develops that is a problem, just call me. But I'm sure everything will be fine." With this arrangement I would be free to work with my other clients. I didn't have to know about each change that was being made.

Teddy was given a bottle and placed in the car seat as Katie turned and said, "I think I would like the wood at the front of the house over the front door to go horizontally not vertically as it does on the model."

I assured her, "That can be easily arranged. It has nothing to do with the structure." I felt sure that this would work out beautifully. We said our good-byes.

I stayed awhile to talk with Terry. I informed her that the buyers had a building supply business in Jersey City. It is a stone's throw from New York City, which is in the midst of a building explosion. They are able to quickly supply the contractor's needs in the city. The business was growing by leaps and bounds. Their condo was paid for. I told Terry I would keep in touch and asked her to call me if I could help in any way. We spoke many times, during the next four weeks, about what was being added and the upgrades. These items did not change the price on which my commission would be based. This $340,000 home was the most expensive transaction in my twenty-year career! I was thrilled. Five weeks slipped by and finally I had a contract in my file, with all the necessary signatures. I just had to wait for the house to be completed and the closing date decided to receive my commission. After all, that is what selling real estate is all about.

The buyers were living in their town house, which they did not have to sell prior to purchasing. Most buyers are not that fortunate. The builder started to excavate for the foundation and basement. There was one other house being built. Whenever I had the opportunity I would stop to see what progress was being made. In a few weeks the house was almost completely framed. I called Terry each week. Everything seemed to be on schedule, but as yet, we had no closing date. The house was completed in about four months.

Terry was no longer there. She had been working for the builder but now a local realtor had acquired the listing for the remainder of the tract. Occasionally, I would meet Tony, the builder, and inquire about the closing date. It was always the same reply, "Don't worry, everything will be fine." There was only one other house built and occupied. Four months had slipped by and I did not know what the holdup was. At this point, since I was not able to get a definite answer from Tony, I decided to contact his attorney. This was not easy. Terry had worked out all the details of the contract with the attorney and the builder. With that arrangement everything should have worked smoothly. But I detected a problem. I finally decided to call Katie and Greg's attorney to obtain the name and number of Tony's attorney. To my great surprise I was told they no longer represented my buyers. To say the least I was shocked. Now I had no alternative. I had to call Katie to find out exactly what was happening. I had not spoken to her in about three weeks.

She was at her office and after a few pleasantries I said, "What's happening? I know the house is completed, but why haven't I gotten a closing date yet?"

"Oh so much has happened. We saw that the house was finished and spoke to our lawyer about a closing because we wanted to know when to put the condo up for sale." She paused for a moment, "He told us it would be soon. We put the condo on the market." She took a deep breath, "It sold immediately. It is a gorgeous condo."

I interrupted with, "What happened to your attorney?"

"When I called and told him we had sold the condo he said, 'You shouldn't have done that.'"

"Why?"

"Then, he told me there was a problem with the closing. I fired him on the spot."

I wanted to get to the bottom of why there was a problem with the closing. "Who is your attorney now?"

"Jim Asher."

"How did you get to this attorney?"

"A friend of mine recommended him to me."

"Katie, Jim is the same real estate attorney I suggested to you eight months ago. You told me you wanted to use a college classmate of your brother's."

"I like Jim very much. We just did this three weeks ago. I think he will work something out for us."

"When is the closing for the condo scheduled?"

"We have three months."

I said I wanted to speak with the builder's attorney and would get back to her.

I called Jim and obtained a little more information. The bank had defaulted but was in the process of being taken over by one of the eminently successful larger banks. In 1988 there were many banks that were overextended and the government eventually bailed them out.

I now had the name of Tony's attorney and was able to reach that office. I left a message asking to be called in reference to the closing. It seemed both the builder and his attorney were trying to avoid me. I called repeatedly and left messages. Getting the attorney to call back was another story. Little by little I obtained disturbing information. I knew that the bank holding his construction loan had gone, as they say, "belly up." This meant no more money for the builder. There was an additional problem. The development was spread into three separate towns, each with different requirements for construction and occupancy.

The one town would not allow occupancy without a pumping station being built first. Katie's house was not in that town. When I finally was able to speak to the builder's attorney she was very evasive. She told me what I already knew about the bank and the pumping station. She added,

"The new bank will evaluate the builder's financial situation and decide on the status of the construction loan." I had never been part of a situation like this. I kept in touch with Tony's attorney feeling that there was where the newest, pertinent information would come from.

Three more months slipped by. I was busy with other buyers. Each month my broker would ask me for the status of that property. She told me, "Hang in there. You have a good rapport with the attorneys; they will keep you informed."

"After all this time I just want to be sure to get my commission. It has been seven months since I showed them the houses." She was sympathetic but had no suggestions.

On another visit to the site, much to my amazement, I observed that Katie's house was occupied! I was beside myself. Had there been a closing? Why had I not been notified? Had I been done out of my commission? Who was living in the house? I decided to go to the door and ring the bell. I got out of the car and started up the steps. What was I going to say to whoever opened the door? I rang the bell and waited. "Why are you living in Katie's house?" No, I couldn't say that. I rang again and waited. No one was at home. I was a little disappointed and a little relieved too.

At my office I once again called the builder's attorney. I found out she was on leave for the birth of her baby. No one told me this before. My calls just weren't answered. I guessed because of the complications with this property, no one wanted to get involved.

I decided to persist, "May I please speak to whoever is handling the Hill Top Estates?" I finally got to speak with someone other than the receptionist. I explained the facts and my interest in the situation. I was again told that the bank had gone into default. I was assured that the new bank, which was taking over, would allow the builder to proceed with the construction. Then this person said, "The buyers are living in the house."

I was stunned with this news! He explained that the buyer's attorney had made arrangements with the builder for them to occupy the house because their town house had been sold. I thought this was a smart move on Tony's part. If Katie and Greg could not move into the house they had a contract on, they would be forced to buy something else. The town agreed to allow a temporary certificate of occupancy to be issued. The other community wanted a pumping station set up before any additional building could proceed. There were lots of unanswered questions in my mind. I decided to stop at the house and speak to Katie. I rang the doorbell. I guess we were both surprised to see each other. We hadn't talked in over a month.

"You are living here! I saw the lights on and the car in the driveway. I wondered what was going on."

"Come in. I have so much to tell you."

The house was fully decorated "yuppie style," with lovely sculpted carpets that picked up the colors of the drapes and the walls. The extra spindles were on the stairs just as she wanted. The kitchen, with the green marble, was gorgeous, opening into the great room. The bath was luxurious. The jacuzzi had two marble steps with room for candles and a glass of wine. There was a nursery next to the master bedroom. A darling little baby girl was sleeping there. "Katie I didn't know you had a baby!"

"It's been two years since we first saw this house. A lot can happen."

The basement was in the process of being finished with a guest area and a children's playroom. We laughed and finished the tour of her home. It was a show place! I complimented her on the color scheme and the selection of furnishings.

"Tell me how you are able to live here and do all these improvements without owning the house?"

"When we saw this place was almost finished, we put our town house on the market. It was a surprise when it sold so quickly. We told Tony we had to have a place to live. I almost called you to see if there was something else we could look at." The phone rang and we were interrupted for a few minutes. "You do know about the bank and the pumping station?" I shook my head. "Tony thought while the new bank was checking out the feasibility of granting the construction mortgage, it would be to his benefit to have the two finished houses occupied. It would give the appearance of interest in the subdivision." She asked me to have a seat and offered me an iced tea.

"How close to getting the construction loan is he?"

"Well we don't get too many answers, other than 'it will work out.'" We both laughed at this; they were getting to be the famous last words.

"What does your lawyer tell you?"

"Not too much."

"Are you happy with Jim?"

"Yes, he's the one who convinced Tony to let us move in here."

Now I began to feel a little more confident about the outcome of this whole prolonged situation. I knew he was very competent. They would have a clear title at the closing. If there was any chance of my office obtaining our commission, I knew he would ensure that. He is a very honest and efficient attorney.

Katie informed me, "We are going to see him tomorrow. I hope he will be able to get to the end of this for all of us."

"I guess we will have to wait to see how the bank feels about the feasibility of this subdivision. When I first showed it to you, I was confident that this concept would work. I felt it would be very lucrative for the developer. He just ran into a little trouble, none of it his doing."

We agreed there was very little we could do except leave it in the hands of the attorneys for the buyers, the sellers, and the banks. Before I left we promised to keep each other informed of any new events.

I went about my business of listing and selling real estate with periodic calls to the lawyers and the buyers. At times I felt that I was being shuffled from one attorney to another and getting nowhere. Then when I would hear those words, "It won't be long now, we are making good progress," I would be energized again. I'd think, "Soon I'll receive the biggest commission I have ever made." Over three years had gone by. The buyers had been living in the house that I found for them, not paying rent, mortgage, or taxes for two years. What a wonderful position to be in. I was hanging in the wind. Every few months my broker would ask, "Anything happening on that closing yet?"

About this time there was a rumor circulating that a big-time builder, one who was on the stock exchange, was showing an interest in the subdivision. There had been many bank foreclosures in the Northeast, and this builder had been very successful in acquiring properties at auction. He had completed some lovely subdivisions and went on to market them very profitably for the stockholders. Katie and Greg were hoping the new builder would continue building houses in the same price range as theirs or perhaps even more expensive homes. This would mean that their home would maintain its purchase price and hopefully increase in value.

They had invested money in a house they did not own, for the decorating, custom carpets, drapes, and a finished basement. They were very anxious and were questioning whether they could walk away from the deal after adding up all the expenses. Would they come out even or ahead, since they had not paid rent, taxes, or a mortgage for two years? Katie and I talked about the possibility of the new builder taking over. They loved their house. The location was perfect and the area was great. Everything about the house pleased them, except the uncertainty of what would be built on the remaining lots. So, it was a waiting game.

The Three-year Contract

Two weeks after our conversation, I heard the new builder was thinking of constructing condominiums practically in Katie and Greg's backyard! I knew they definitely would not be happy about that. This drawn-out transaction had made me feel like a yo-yo. It had now been three years since I previewed what I thought was the perfect house for my wonderful cash buyers. A bank had gone into default, a builder had gone bankrupt, a family had been living free for two years, and I had been waiting for a commission.

I had not given up. I had followed through. I had kept in touch with all the parties. These are the golden rules of real estate. The phone rang. It was Katie's husband. He told me that the big builder, the one on the stock exchange, had finally completed all of their paperwork. He was the new owner of the subdivision and would continue to build homes in the four- to five-hundred-thousand-dollar price range.

"We are having our closing in three weeks!"

I congratulated him. We talked about all the delays and uncertainties. We laughed about how many times, over three years, we had heard, "Don't worry, everything will work out." He ended by saying how much they really loved the house and how they appreciated that I had kept on top of everything.

There had been so much confusion and delay, but I was finally able to take a deep breath and relax over this complex transaction. I decided to call their attorney.

"It's all settled!" Jim said. "Don't worry, everything will work out." This time I truly believed those words. Jim assured me the check would be at the office on the day of the closing and it was.

Did someone say, "Selling real estate is a quick and easy way to make money?"

CHAPTER 11

No Mortgage

And then there was the couple who zeroed in on a house they both liked. The following day the wife came in to take a second look. Thinking it was time to talk about filling out a mortgage application, I started to ask a few questions. "Where is your husband employed?"

"Oh—he has his own business."

"When will he be able to come in to fill out a mortgage application?"

"We intend to pay cash."

She left me twenty new one hundred dollar bills as part of the earnest money. Later that day they both came in to sign the contract. He reassured me they would not require a mortgage. We spoke many times before the closing. All the inspections were completed without any problems.

The afternoon of the closing they came to the attorney's office with $110,000 *cash* in a brown paper bag. Counting out the money was an experience! We were all shocked to see so much *cash*; it was in fifty- and one-hundred-dollar bills. The attorneys excused themselves and went into another room. I was not privy as to how they worked this out.

Eighteen months later we saw his name in the newspaper, associated with a waterfront mob in New York City.

CHAPTER 12

Move Number Nine

Who in their right mind would move nine times in twenty-five years? That's a move every two or three years! It might be understandable if you were in the military service, but I was not. Money made me do it.

In 1972, I was estranged from my husband. We were still living in the family residence, yet living apart. The year before this had occurred, I started my real estate career. Selling real estate is a very demanding business. My son would say, "Take the phone off the hook so you can finish dinner." Working seven days a week is not unusual. Evening hours can be taken up with phone calls and appointments, but this was not the reason for my marital breakup.

I worked very hard, putting in many hours. I was able to save all the money I earned because the children and I were living together and their father was paying the household bills. When all my friends were wearing designer labels, I was sewing blouses and skirts for myself. A year and a half after this stressful living situation I had saved enough money for a down payment on an estate fixer-upper house. The house was empty for over a year. It had belonged to an elderly couple who had no children. It was built in 1920. With the help of a friend who was familiar with the old-time farm families in the neighborhood, we were able to locate the bank handling the estate. It was several counties away. I called the bank's president and asked for an appointment to talk with him about the Haine's property. He was agreeable and the next afternoon I was in his office. I felt a little intimidated. I had never met him before. It was a wealthy town and the bank reflected this in the office furnishings and the lovely rich paneling. I had heard that the price was twenty-five thousand dollars. He asked if I had found my way to the bank easily and how long the drive had taken. Then we started to talk about the property. I said, "The house needs a lot of work. It has a coal stove for heat and the kitchen is ancient."

His response was, "It's a very well built house and in a very nice area."

"I'm prepared to offer twenty thousand dollars." I was hoping to pay less than the bank wanted. "I will have to invest at least twenty thousand for a new kitchen and bath, heating system, decorating, and landscaping." I held my breath and thought he would take his time and think this over. I was wrong.

"Twenty-five thousand is what we are looking for."

Every thousand I could save would help with the renovations. "Twenty-four thousand," I said.

He pushed his chair away and I knew the meeting was over. I quickly said, "Alright, twenty-five thousand dollars." He reached out to shake my hand while he nodded his head yes.

"The heirs decided, just yesterday, that twenty-five thousand was the rock bottom price they would accept."

"I will mail the contract to you tomorrow." I was so happy I felt weightless.

"With a deposit too," he reminded me. It turned out to be a very pleasant meeting, but I never saw him again.

As I drove back I thought, "I have to get started with a mortgage, a builder, and a heating contractor. Boy, selling a house to myself is different than selling to a stranger." The next day I put the contract together and mailed it, with a check, to the seller's bank.

In 1973 when I told my friends I was buying a house the response was, "You're a woman on your own. You will never get a mortgage." That was the encouragement I received. But that was the reality of the day. The divorce rate was very low.

Married couples bought houses together. Unmarried couples didn't even think about purchasing together. My friends didn't understand how determined I was to have my own home. They were unaware of the business connections I had established in the last two and a half years.

I went to see the president of a local bank where I had taken many of my buyers to apply for their mortgages. I explained my marital situation to Hendrick and my plans to renovate the old boarded up house. He seemed interested in helping me and told me to fill out a mortgage application. I did this and left the information with him. I contacted a builder whom I had worked with in the past. I needed an estimate on the renovations and improvements I planned to have done, to figure what my expenses would be. I did the same with heating contractors. The husband of my real estate broker was a painter. His price was wonderful. I had all my figures together.

A few weeks later Hendrick called and asked me to come into his office. When I arrived I saw he had a very serious look on his face and a handful of papers.

"How does everything look?" I asked, hoping for a positive answer.

"There are a lot of judgments against you."

I was shocked. In the three years that I had been working I paid all my bills on time. I had two charge accounts that I paid in full at the end of each month.

"I can't understand this. I pay all my bills on time. Nothing is outstanding." He handed me the credit report. There was so much to read on the five pages that I was confused. My eyes were filled with tears and it was hard to read. I didn't see my name anyplace but where my two charge accounts were listed.

"Hendrick, these aren't against me. They are all against my soon-to-be ex-husband and his business. We're in the middle of a divorce."

Move Number Nine

We looked at the report together. I pointed out that the charge accounts with Sears and Hahnes were in my name only. "You can see that they have been paid on time for the past three years." I was still hopeful that I could obtain a mortgage. My heart was pounding. I was very nervous. This was my first attempt to transact financial business on my own.

He thought for a while and said, "In order for you to obtain a mortgage, the board of directors will insist that your estranged spouse sign off all rights to this property." He looked at me very sympathetically, and said, "Do you think he will?"

My mind went into a tailspin: "Will he agree to this? If he doesn't, what will I be able to do? Is this the end of my chance to get in on a good opportunity?" I got my thoughts together and said, "I'll tell him he has to do it. There's no other way to get a mortgage." He wished me luck and I left. I felt very let down. Mentally, I started to rehearse what I would say to John. I had to be careful. He was a very calculating person.

That night we discussed the problem. I told him, "Your credit is causing a problem with my ability to qualify for the loan." As I suspected he was not ready to accept the decision I wanted him to make.

In a very authoritarian way he said, "I'll check with a few other banks that I've had contacts with."

He was not going to give up easily. I guess he wanted to show me he was still in control. I never did know if he actually contacted any banks or if he was trying to make me feel insecure. After a few very anxious days, that included a long weekend, he signed away all his rights to the property. I was ecstatic.

Since we were still married, even though the down payment was money I had earned, he could have claimed half ownership of the property. I took the papers to Hendrick. He informed me that the board would meet the following week and I would have my answer then. I was very tense all week, wondering if I would qualify. The house was in a prime area of town. If I ever wanted to sell it, I knew there would be no problem. The profit would be all mine.

A week later the phone rang and I heard, "Your mortgage has been approved."

"Thank you. Thank you very much!" What a feeling! Suddenly I recalled the words said to me three months ago by an acquaintance: "You won't get a mortgage; you're a woman alone."

The banking laws and restrictions were different at that time. I was dealing with a privately owned bank and I was able to obtain a mortgage for 100 percent of the sales price. The agreement was that I would put the down payment into the renovation of the property. That was how I bought my first home. I was one of the first working women in the area to obtain a mortgage.

With that first property I had the opportunity to work with a number of subcontractors. What a learning experience that was! I obtained a few estimates for a new heating system, and made arrangements to have the old coal furnace and the coal bin, that still had coal in it, removed. The heating contractor didn't want to make the removal part of his estimate. That was the first problem. How do you look in the yellow pages for "coal remover"?

The kitchen was fifty-seven years old and very small; by using the rear porch I was able to enlarge the size of the kitchen. I designed the kitchen layout. My preference is to have a window over the kitchen sink and the stove and sink close to each other. I shopped for cabinets to find something I liked and to get the best buy. The pantry was turned into a first floor bathroom. Most older homes in the area did not have this luxury. The second floor bathroom was an ancient disaster. It didn't even have a shower! I redesigned it by moving the location of the tub and the sink. There was a long window right next to the Johnny. I didn't relish sitting there,

Move Number Nine   107

with the light on, for my neighbors to see me. I replaced it with a smaller window for privacy. The modernized version was lovely. I selected the wallpaper and paint for the interior and exterior. A neutral wall-to-wall carpet was installed over pine floors. All the bills were paid; just the mortgage was hanging over my head.

I coordinated my office time, my buyers and sellers, and the subcontractors for two months while this project was being completed. Living conditions at "home" were difficult. I hadn't told anyone I was moving into the renovated property. I implied that I was not sure if I would sell it. When the last subcontractor had finished his work, I started calling moving companies for estimates. Now that my son and his father were in business together and my daughter was away at college, I felt very insecure at "home." I wondered how I could move out and not have an argument or hear verbal threats. In a whisper I said to myself, "I will not tell anyone. I'll just do it."

I hired the mover for a Friday because that was payday for my soon-to-be ex-husband's employees, which meant he would not be home. Moving time was arranged. It had to be after he left for work. I never knew when he would leave since he had his own business. Often he would come home unexpectedly. Boy was that bizarre! As soon as he left I went to the supermarket to find sturdy empty cartons. When the movers came in the front door I started to fill the cartons with dishes, pots, pans, utensils, and all the other things I would need. I was never so nervous in my entire life! I kept looking out the window to see if I was going to be caught in the act of moving. But it worked out!

On several occasions, we had discussed the division of the household property in the event either of us moved out. I took only what I said I would take. Maybe that's not 100 percent true. A few days later, I returned and took the washer and the gas dryer. This action could have had disastrous repercussions. The father of my children was a plumbing and heating contractor always looking for a shortcut. He had not installed a shut-off valve at the gas connection for the dryer. The inexperienced young man helping me move the washer and dryer did not know anything about gas, electric, or plumbing. Neither did I. We just disconnected the dryer and took it to my new home. Oh, I put a cork in the end of the gas pipeline.

That evening I had a phone call. "What the hell is the matter with you?"

"What are you talking about?"

"I smelled gas when I came in the garage tonight. You could have blown up the whole damn house!"

"If you had put in a shut-off valve, there would not have been a problem." I think I hung up.

All went well, for about three years. The finished renovations were lovely. The compliments were nice to receive. My daughter lived with me while attending a local college. Gradually in the late 1970s real estate took a bad turn. I was not able to make as many sales as in previous months. As this was happening my ex-husband abruptly stopped my alimony payments. I decided that an income property might work better for me. My lovely refurbished house was put on the market. I enjoyed it while I could afford the expenses. My first house sold immediately for a very nice profit. I doubled my investment.

A large older one-family house that had been converted into a two-family house came on the market. I made a bid on it. After some negotiating we arrived at an acceptable price. Hendrick, again, helped me in obtaining my second mortgage. I had no problems with the next six mortgages I applied for. The "no mortgage for women" syndrome had disappeared. This two-family house was the same vintage as my former home with lovely wood trim and a fireplace. New kitchen cabinets were installed in my kitchen and the small old kitchen in the rental apartment. The contractors came to do the decorating, wallpapering, and to install the wall-to-wall carpet. When finished it was very attractive. The rent did help with the expenses. I made attractive drapes for the windows and arranged wall decorations in interesting designs. All this added to the charm of my home.

I enjoyed living there for two years. Then I decided I wanted something better. I was not sure if I wanted to stay in the area or make a complete change to a new town. A realtor friend offered me the opportunity to join her office. The location was in a wonderful ocean-side community a few hours away. The town was very affluent. The prices of the homes were triple compared to where I had been selling. Since I had done very well in real estate at my original location, I expected my success to continue.

I listed my home for sale. Once again property prices had increased. The value of my home had almost doubled. I was able to make a good profit on this sale also.

About this time one of my friends said, "You are ruining my address book. The whole page is full of *your* addresses."

"Write the new address in pencil, then you can erase it, because there will be more moves," was my comment.

This move was a mistake. Mortgage money dried up, buyers were not rushing to make offers as they had when money was readily available. Mortgage rates escalated to 16 and 17 percent during this time! Buyers disappeared. I was still receiving commission checks from the sales I had finalized at my former broker's office. This was a tremendous help. In addition to a dead market I began to have tremendous problems with my former husband, in regard to the divorce settlement. He reneged on an agreement concerning a life insurance policy, on which he was to pay the premiums. At the same time he also tried to involve me in a bank loan he had obtained for his business. When his bank contacted me about the loan, which was due, I guess I became paranoid. I thought they might be able to attach my accounts.

This was the money I worked so hard to acquire and save. I had pulled wallpaper from old walls, washed windows, cleaned out junk that dead owners had left in empty houses. I even planted the shrubs myself so I could save money. One day I was so consumed with anxiety that I went to the two banks I had my accounts in and transferred the accounts to two other banks. Fear was consuming me. I had difficulty sleeping. Could they really take my money from me? I had not signed for that loan! After a few months of being on edge I decided to return to my home base, where I had established many contacts through the years.

The bank's attorneys were in touch with me. There was a meeting, a very tense meeting. John was late. After a very emotional session, it was decided I had not signed the loan agreement. Once this was settled I was very relieved.

After interviewing a few real estate agencies, I decided on a small well-established office in the town I had started out in. A large garden apartment rental complex was my new residence. At this time, New Jersey had not yet accepted the condominium concept of home ownership. Suddenly, in one of the nearby communities, condos were being built. Everyone was excited. Young, first-time homebuyers were flocking to the new condos. The prices were less than on a small older house. All the modern conveniences were available; central air, dishwashers, garbage disposals, washers, and dryers. Before long several other towns were issuing permits for condos. Even older rental garden apartments were being converted to condo ownership. The owners of the apartment I lived in decided to convert. The tenants were given a "first option" at a discounted insider's price if they wished to purchase. I decided to be a buyer. In fact, I bought two at the insider's price. I sold the one I was living in and doubled my money. I moved to the second condo, which had a lovely setting. It looked out on green grass and flowering trees. I lived there for two years before my next move. Once again the location, condition, and great decorating made the sale quick and profitable. At this point I realized how fortunate I was to be able to move whenever the opportunity occurred. I had no one to account to but myself.

The market was steadily improving. I thought condo ownership was a very good concept. I located five pieces of property that were adjacent to each other and zoned for condominiums. I contacted each owner and tried to convince them to sell. It was not easy. One property was an estate. The house belonged to the son of a deceased woman. Before his brother had died he lived there with his wife. The sister-in-law had come from Italy two years before. She did not speak English and did not work. It was a very difficult decision for the former brother-in-law to make. He was finally able to relocate his dead brother's wife and agreed to sell. After a few months I was successful in convincing all the owners to sell.

I had one buyer interested in all of the properties. It turned out to be the last large piece of property in Glen Ridge and the first condominium to be built. The buyer offered me the opportunity to become the listing agent for the thirty-six units in the three-story condominium. The architect-builder designed a lovely contemporary building. It was of modular construction, another new concept for the building industry. I placed a hold on one of the two-bedroom condominiums prior to construction. At that time the builder was offering them at a discount. As construction of the new condos neared completion, I decided it was time to put the condo I was living in up for sale. The sale was quick. This investment almost tripled!

Shortly after I moved in, all the units in the new condo were sold. We made a very nice profit on this venture. I earned the most money ever that year. That was when I started my investment portfolio. I enjoyed living there, mortgage free, for three years.

Once again, about 1990, the market was changing. Large corporations were consolidating. Jobs were unsure. These were the days when President Bush was in office. Real estate sales fell off. Buyers were not as anxious or as numerous as before. The economy slowed down. I began to think about another career, but what? I loved this business. Real estate had been good to me. Why give up now?

I decided to put my condo up for sale. At the open house everyone loved it, but no buyers. After six months there were still no buyers. I took it off the market. The taxes were very high, $3,700 for nine hundred square feet of living space. The following spring I put it on the market again with the same results. The condo market was not good. It is always the first

Move Number Nine

market to slow down and the last to respond in an upswing.

Finally there was someone interested. A coworker said, "How lucky!"

"But she's offering ten thousand dollars less than I want."

Kathy is down-to-earth and speaks her mind. "How many offers have you had?"

She knew the answer. "None."

"In this market that ought to tell you something. Grab it!"

At that time many homeowners who were forced to sell were caught in a bind. The prices on real estate had dropped so low that often the selling price did not cover the balance of their mortgage. They were getting less for their home than they had paid for it. They lost money.

I said, "I really wanted more money."

"You're like all the sellers. They always want more money too. Take it!"

This turned out to be the best advice anyone had ever given to me. It sold for one and a half times the price I paid! In a bad market this was fantastic. To my knowledge none of the other comparable units have sold anywhere near my price. I moved again to a small older rental garden apartment.

In twenty-five years, real estate has shown me up markets and down markets, high and low interest rates. It can be a feast or famine business. Long hours when you are busy and making money, and longer hours when you are not making money, because you are afraid to leave the office for fear you might miss something important about a sale or vital to a listing. Vacations were planned and vacations were delayed, because a buyer or a seller decided to take action. My lease on the apartment lasted just under three years.

My daughter who lives in Franklin, Tennessee, outside of Nashville had been after me for years to move to Franklin. On each visit I wondered, "Why go back to the congested, crowded, overpriced, overtaxed New Jersey area that I call home?" Nashville is a very interesting city. There is so much more to enjoy than just country music. For the sports-minded there are the Tennessee Titans football team and the Nashville Predators ice hockey team. The arts are represented by the Nashville Symphony, Ballet, and Opera. The restaurants are wonderful: American, Italian, Japanese, Greek, and Southern, and most are informal. A few of the very expensive ones are more formal. To my friends I describe Nashville as a little New York City. Whatever you want, it is here!

In Franklin there are rolling hills, valleys, and miles and miles of green farmland. In the fall and summer the foliage is beautiful. The center of town is an old-fashioned county square. The old colonial homes have been restored and are maintained beautifully. On some of the back one-lane roads you can drive for twenty minutes and never meet another car. So, on a visit with Debbie, we checked out a few rental apartments. They really know how to build beautiful garden apartments in Nashville! All the modern amenities are included. The landscaping is generous, colorful, so well kept, and inviting.

I decided to move again! Construction on the apartment I selected would be completed in two months. The new apartment was larger than what I had in New Jersey, with central air, two bedrooms, and two bathrooms. The wall-to-wall carpet and venetian blinds were included plus a touch of wallpaper in the kitchen. The rent was twenty-five dollars a month less than I paid for an old one bedroom, one bathroom apartment in New Jersey. Food shopping and the mall were five minutes away. It was perfect to start out with in a new community.

When the decision was made to move, I told my family and friends in New Jersey of my plans. They were all very surprised. At the office I turned over my buyers and sellers to competent associates. There were luncheons, good-bye parties, and gifts. It was all very exciting. In between all this, boxes were being packed in a leisurely fashion. It was far different from that first move when I left the "family" home.

My son-in-law flew north to drive back to Tennessee with me. We made the trip in one day. It was a long fifteen-hour

Move Number Nine

experience. We drove in my new car and the movers followed a week later. They ruined my furniture, but that's another story. I settled in and made a few new friends. In January it snowed one day, but it was gone in twenty-four hours—so different from New Jersey.

The one-year lease on my apartment in Nashville soon expired. Needless to say I had been looking at the beautiful homes in Franklin. I guess it was natural to gravitate toward my daughter's location. Not too close, but conveniently nearby. I don't have a real estate license in Tennessee, but I am affiliated with a national referral brokerage office. I met with a very informed and competent saleswoman. The area is lovely: a golf course with a few lakes, rolling hills, flowering trees, and pretty brick homes. They even have pansies that bloom all winter! In a few weeks we inspected eight houses.

I really wanted a ranch. Since we could not find one, and I wanted to stay in this location, I decided to make an offer on a colonial. It was larger than I needed but I could spread out and have room for visitors. After much negotiating, the price was settled. The taxes were wonderful! In New Jersey on a comparable house taxes would be twelve to thirteen thousand dollars a year. The taxes on this seven-room colonial with three bedrooms and three bathrooms are $1,323 a year! Is it any wonder that Tennessee is so popular?

Here comes move number *nine*! Real estate has been good to me, so why should I give up on it now? I'm buying a house on a golf course. I was able to get it at a very fair price because the house was neglected. One of real estate's best-kept secrets is, "Don't buy the best house in the neighborhood." Large corporations are gravitating to this city. Gorgeous new homes are bought before they are completely built. Nashville and Franklin are booming! The new millennium has arrived! Real estate is flourishing. I'm getting in on a good thing!

I always enjoy a challenge and moving *is* a challenge. Once again I was hiring contractors to do the painting, floor refinishing, door lock replacements, carpet and window cleaning, and pest control. Putting it all together is an adventure but not as difficult as the first house I bought and renovated. Now I can afford to hire subcontractors to do even the small jobs.

The "no mortgage for women" syndrome has long disappeared. Everyone is not up to this sort of thing. But I knew a long time ago when I "secretly" moved from the family home I would succeed. I was not going to be divorced and poor.

I've moved into my new home, and it looks wonderful. The golf course view is beautiful and restful. I have even learned to play the game.

Is this the final move? Is number ten coming up? I like a challenge and if I can make some money, why not? Money made me do it before!

The End

About the Author

Lucille Palis Finamore graduated from Bloomfield High School in New Jersey, then went on to become a dental nurse. She was married during the Second World War.

While living in Anniston, Alabama, she trained to be a nurse's aid. At the end of the war she and her husband designed and built their starter home.

Five years into the marriage she was finally pregnant. Michael James was born on April 26, 1951, and three years later Deborah Mary came into their lives on March 17, 1954.

Lucille designed her third house. It was built in Glen Ridge, New Jersey, adjacent to the Glen Ridge Country Club.

When Lucille was fifty years old, at a time when most women were happy being housewives and stay-at-home mothers, she divorced her husband of twenty-five years. She then became a real estate associate. Lucille successfully sold real estate for twenty-five years, invested wisely, bought, renovated, and sold her properties.

In Nashville, Tennessee, she attended "Retirement Learning" at Vanderbilt University. An instructor encouraged her to pursue publication of her writing.

Lucille Palis Finamore currently resides in Franklin, Tennessee, where she enjoys playing golf, bridge, volunteering, and writing.